HONORING OUR NEIGHBOR'S FAITH

Augsburg Fortress

CONTENTS

Honoring Our Neighbor's Faith
A resource supporting the ELCA's Initiatives for a New Century.

General Editor: Robert Buckley Farlee
Edited by Mark Gardner and Douglas Schmitz
Cover and interior designed by Krogstad Design Inc.
Interior art by Markell Studios

ISBN 0-8066-3846-X

Manufactured in U.S.A.
1 2 3 4 5 6 7 8 9 0 1 2 3 4 5 6 7 8 9

INTRODUCTION

This resource invites us to honor our neighbor's faith. That is, it acknowledges the obvious, that different people—especially in pluralistic America—have different beliefs, and those beliefs are worthy of respect. It is difficult, though, to respect that which we do not understand. Indeed, we have seen all too often that disrespect, distrust, and fear of other religious traditions often stems from simple misunderstanding. This is an age-old problem, and Christians have been both perpetrators and victims of such misunderstanding. Early Christians were accused of cannibalism because of confusion regarding the Lord's Supper. Present-day Muslims are thought, all too commonly, to support "holy war" against Christians. Even within the Christian camp, perceptions of other denominations often travel far from reality.

Here, religious groups are allowed to tell their own story: who they are, what they believe, and how they practice. In many cases, writers from within the traditions agreed to write the articles. In all cases, the chapters were sent to representatives of the groups for their review. We have tried to be fair toward their beliefs, attempting in our editing not to put our slant on their faith. The exception is in the discussion questions, where we encourage Lutherans and others who use this resource to evaluate the various beliefs in light of their own faith.

That leads us to the flip side of this particular coin: the existence of another faith means that it is different from our own faith. How do we deal with that variance in beliefs? Yes, we honor our neighbor's faith and trust that it is as heartfelt as our own, but where do we go from there? If we are Lutheran, presumably we believe that the Lutheran understanding of God is the most correct. How, then, do we approach the beliefs of other faith groups—are they equally correct, just different? Are they misguided but essentially okay? Are they flat-out wrong? To put it differently, do we agree with those who would say that all religious traditions are equally valid understandings of the universal God, or do we agree with those who would insist that Christianity—or, more narrowly, our flavor of Christianity—is the *only* way to approach God?

These are difficult questions and are answered in many ways. Some Christians will not pray with others whom they acknowledge to be Christian. Other Christians are willing to accept as valid the beliefs of those who have never pretended to be Christian. Still other Christians struggle to deal with groups who bear some trappings of Christianity while departing from some basic Christian teachings. But tricky and sometimes wrenching as these questions are, we can be certain that satisfactory answers cannot be found by ignoring or misrepresenting what other faith traditions believe. We need to gain accurate information and to examine that information respectfully. We must compare what we learn with our own beliefs, and that means we must have a solid understanding of what our own faith asks of us.

That is the process this book seeks to facilitate. We don't expect that all will come to an agreement on who God is and how we should practice our beliefs, even among Christian denominations. It is hoped, though, that we can gain sympathetic knowledge about what others believe and why, that we can gain some insight from other faiths that may help us in our own faith journeys, and that without dishonoring our own faith in any way, we can honor our neighbor's faith.

Faith Traditions to Be Found Here

Hundreds of different Christian denominations and dozens of non-Christian ones are to be found in North America. Regrettably, we did not have space to include all of them in this resource. We tried to choose groups that would represent a wide spectrum of beliefs, and groups that would represent the majority of "our neighbors' faiths" that readers would be likely to come across. Of course, if there are other faiths you would like to investigate, you are encouraged to do so.

The faith traditions that are discussed here may be placed into four broad categories, but in some cases you will have to decide on the category for a given group. The first category is *world religions unrelated to Christianity*. This is fairly clear, comprising the ancient religions of Hinduism (or Vedanta) and Buddhism. Second, *non-Christian world religions with a "family" connection to Christianity*. Again, no confusion here: Judaism is the source from which Christianity developed, and Islam is a later religion from the same roots. The last two categories are where different people will make different calls: *Christian denominations* and *non-Christian denominations with Christian roots*. Few observers would question that Episcopalians or Methodists are Christian. There are some other denominations, though, that may claim to be Christian but whose beliefs may, for some, put that identification in question. Read the essays, look at the Tables of Comparison, and try to make your own call.

A Note about Procedure

Users are free to make use of this resource as best fits their circumstances. A minimal approach might be to read through each chapter (perhaps pairing up some of the shorter ones) and discuss them, beginning with the questions provided. In some cases classes may wish to expand on these presentations with class members researching further into the history and beliefs of various groups. Where possible, it could be enlightening to invite someone from each tradition to come and speak to your class, and a trip to visit the worship of the group under discussion could be the best way to get a feel for who they are. If you plan to do such a visit, it is polite to contact the local group ahead of time, find out if there are any restrictions on dress or behavior, and learn any hints to help you get more out of your visit. They may be able to have someone serve as a host for your group. A noteworthy resource for doing such visiting is *How to Be a Perfect Stranger: A Guide to Etiquette in Other People's Religious Ceremonies,* edited by Arthur J. Magida and Stuart M. Matlins, 2 vols. (Woodstock, Vt.: Jewish Lights Publishing, 1996, 1997).

Initiatives for a New Century

This resource was developed with the support and encouragement of the "Teach the Faith Initiative Team" as part of the ELCA Initiatives for a New Century. The 1997 ELCA churchwide assembly affirmed the following commitment as part of this church's response to teaching the faith:

> *We will learn about our faith and our Lutheran understanding of Scripture by exploring both our differences and our similarities with other faith traditions. From the perspective of the Eighth Commandment we will ask, "What does it mean to put the best construction on another's faith experience"?*

CHAPTER 1

African American Methodist Churches

Richard Allen (1760–1831), the founder and first bishop of the African Methodist Episcopal Church, grew up as a slave in Philadelphia.

You probably will not come across a congregation claiming to belong to the "African American Methodist" church body. Rather, this is an umbrella term for a number of denominations that have become very important, particularly in the African American community. They include the African Methodist Episcopal Church (A.M.E.), the African American Episcopal Zion Church, the Christian Methodist Episcopal Church, the Union American Methodist Church, Inc., and the African Union First Colored Methodist Protestant Church.

These churches have their roots in the Methodist Church, which developed under the leadership of John Wesley, an eighteenth century Englishman who led what was at first a reforming movement within the Anglican church. His followers, called "Methodists" first as a mocking term, came to accept the name and spread their teachings throughout the world.

Among those teachings was an emphasis on sanctification, the process by which the Holy Spirit both leads people to faith and continues to develop their relationship to God. Wesley also promoted the concept of the human will being free to make its choices, under the influence of God's grace.

Problems with Discrimination

The Methodist Church became a separate church body in the United States in 1784. While it attracted a wide variety of people, black Christians in particular were drawn to it, in part, because of John Wesley's strong antislavery statements. He denounced the slave trade as being against the will of God. These beliefs at first carried over into the Methodist Church, where no distinctions were made between races, and in fact where members were encouraged to set free any slaves they owned. Unfortunately, as the number of Methodists increased, especially in the South where slavery was seen as an indispensable part of life, the church tended to become less outspoken in opposing slavery. Of course, this wasn't a problem only for Methodists, nor did it occur only in the American South. African Americans in the North experienced discrimination as well.

In reaction to this, it wasn't long before African Americans began pulling out of the mother church to form Methodist congregations, and later denominations, where they would be able to participate fully. The first congregation to withdraw in this way was St. George's Methodist Episcopal Church in Philadelphia in 1787. These actions eventually led to the founding of the African Methodist Episcopal Church in 1816. The African Methodist Episcopal Zion Church was born in 1796, the result of African Americans being denied full participation in a church in New York City. The third of the large African American Methodist bodies was a product of the Reconstruction era following the American Civil War. In 1870, black members of the Methodist Episcopal Church, South, asked to form their own church within the larger denomination. Instead, the parent body voted to constitute them as a completely independent denomination that was called the Christian Methodist Episcopal Church.

Believing and Practicing

Reflecting their history, African American Methodist churches maintain doctrines similar to other Methodist bodies. They are trinitarian, looking to God as the Creator, Jesus Christ as the Son of God and Redeemer of humanity, and the Holy Spirit as the Sanctifier. They teach the sinfulness of humans and their need for repentance, as well as reliance on God's grace for salvation. At the same time, there is a strong expectation that faith in God will lead to lives that reflect the dwelling of the Holy Spirit.

As would be expected, worship in the African American Methodist churches blends Methodist forms with African American styles. The music is generally spirited, including gospel, spirituals, and European-based hymns. A choir usually leads the singing, and may be accompanied by piano, organ, drums, and other instruments.

The word *Episcopal* in the name of most of these denominations means that they are headed by a bishop. This is also the case among other Methodist denominations and reflects their development from an Anglican heritage, as well as biblical roots. Local congregations, however, have a great deal of autonomy in deciding their own forms of ministry.

Members of these churches put their beliefs into practice in their communities. The church is often a center of neighborhood life, and its ministries extend far beyond worship to meeting the everyday needs of the people around them. The church building may be, in turn, a place to feed the hungry, to care for children, to discuss community concerns, and to collect clothing for local or foreign needs. The African American Methodist churches have helped to meet an important need, both historically and in the present day.

For Discussion

□ In what ways is having churches made up primarily of one ethnic heritage (whether it is white, African American, Asian, Hispanic, or some other) helpful? In what ways could it be harmful?

□ Clearly the church sinned when it discriminated against African Americans. Is it free of such problems now?

□ Churches such as the African American Methodist denominations challenge others to become equally involved in their communities. How is your congregation meeting that challenge?

For Further Study

□ *Songs of Zion: The African Methodist Episcopal Church in the U. S. and South Africa* by James T. Campbell (University of North Carolina Press, 1998)

□ Web sites: www.ame-church.org
www.amezion.org

Table of Comparison	*African American Methodists*	*Lutherans*
Teachings	1. Believe the Bible contains the Word of God. 2. Teach justification by faith. 3. Consider Baptism and Holy Communion not only symbolically, but also as signs of God's grace. 4. Believe the church should express its faith in concrete action in the affairs of the world.	1. Accept the Bible as the written witness to God's revelation of saving action through Jesus Christ. 2. Same. 3. Consider Baptism and Holy Communion as God's means of conveying God's grace. 4. Believe the church lives to preach the gospel and celebrate the sacraments, giving strength for service in the world.
Type of Worship	Quite free and emotional, though often based on liturgical patterns.	Liturgical, following the primary pattern of the Western church.
Government	Episcopal, with bishop but no claim to apostolic succession. Congregations quite free within clearly defined channels.	Interdependent congregational, regional, national, and global expressions of the church characterized by democratic decision making, strong ecumenical relationships, elected leadership, and an ordained ministry.
Characteristics	Major emphasis on Christian living as the fruit of personal commitment and clear understanding of Christian doctrine. Predominantly, but not exclusively, African American membership.	Strong emphasis on correct doctrine, with Christian life to proceed from belief as faith becomes active in love. Predominantly, but not exclusively, white membership.
Statistics*	Membership ....5,470,000 Congregations ....13,438 *U. S. statistics of three largest bodies, from *Yearbook of American and Canadian Churches 1998*.	

CHAPTER 2

Assemblies of God

Free and informal worship experiences featuring prayer and praise are characteristic of Assemblies of God congregations.

The Assemblies of God is one of several Pentecostal denominations in the United States. These groups, of which the Assemblies is one of the largest, are comprised of approximately 400 million believers in all parts of the world.

The term *Pentecostal* comes from the experience of Jesus' disciples on Pentecost when the Holy Spirit came upon them (Acts 2). This event has been interpreted in various ways, but Pentecostals understand it as a baptism in the Holy Spirit that brought its recipients certain, special gifts. While this experience continued in the Church from time to time down through history, it reemerged in the early days of the twentieth century with a Pentecostal revival that swept the world and touched all denominations. Many believers began receiving this baptism in the Holy Spirit, including the initial evidence of "speaking in tongues." At first there was no organization; however, in 1914 the Assemblies of God was formed and various other Pentecostal groups also began.

Theologically, the Assemblies of God is *Arminian,* stressing the free will of human beings. It is believed that humankind fell into sin and needs salvation. The believer's part is to repent and believe Christ died for one's sins, then God forgives. In the new birth, at salvation, Jesus Christ comes to dwell by his Spirit within the new believer.

Worship in Assemblies of God churches tends to be informal, with the focus of the service on preaching the Word of God. The Bible is affirmed as verbally inspired of God, and it is the authority for faith and conduct in the life of the Christian. Two ordinances are practiced: water baptism by immersion as a confession of faith after a person has accepted Christ as Savior; and the Lord's supper or communion.

The Assemblies of God does not belong to the World Council or National Council of Churches; however, it is a member of the National Association of Evangelicals, the Pentecostal/Charismatic Churches of North America, the Pentecostal World Conference, and the World Assemblies of God Fellowship.

The church sponsors benevolent/social ministries such as Teen Challenge (a drug rehabilitation program with centers worldwide); children's home, adoption agency, and feeding programs through the local church; and a Convoy of Hope ministry. However, these are not viewed as the major mission of the denomination. Rather, the Assemblies of God is committed to fulfilling a threefold mission: (1) world evangelization; (2) worship to God; and (3) discipleship/training of believers. The church teaches that God, through salvation, is able to change an individual and will thus transform society through changed persons.

For Discussion

□ The Assemblies of God have grown rapidly in recent years. What do you think are some reasons for this growth?
□ Pentecostals place a greater emphasis on certain gifts of the Holy Spirit (see 1 Corinthians 12:4 and following) than do some other Christians. How do you react to that?
□ While Lutherans speak of sacraments as means of grace, the Assemblies of God understand baptism and the Lord's supper as ordinances. How would this difference affect how church members approached these events?

For Further Study

Pamphlets available from Gospel Publishing House:
□ "The Assemblies of God: The Local Church"
□ "The Assemblies of God: Our 16 Doctrines"
□ "The Assemblies of God: Our Distinctive Doctrine"
□ Assemblies of God Web site: www.ag.org

Table of Comparison	*Assemblies of God*	*Lutherans*
Teachings	1. Believe the Bible is the completely inspired Word of God. 2. Practice two ordinances: baptism by immersion and the Lord's supper. 3. Believe in an experience called "baptism in the Holy Spirit" following salvation with speaking in tongues. 4. Accept the triune nature of God and the divinity of Christ. 5. Believe Christ's death provided healing for the body as well as salvation for the soul.	1. Believe the Bible is the written witness to God's revelation of saving action through Jesus Christ. 2. Celebrate two sacraments: Baptism and the Lord's Supper. 3. Believe the Holy Spirit is given in Baptism. Speaking in tongues is the least of the gifts of the Spirit. 4. Same. 5. Bodily healing viewed as usually occurring through normal medical care.
Type of Worship	Free and informal with hymns, prayers, and preaching. Spontaneous testimonies sometimes included.	Orderly liturgical patterns with varying roles for pastors, other lay leaders, and the congregation.
Government	Fellowship of independent congregations organized into districts, usually following state lines.	Interdependent congregational, regional, national, and global expressions of the church characterized by democratic decision making, strong ecumenical relationships, elected leadership, and an ordained ministry.
Characteristics	Emphasis on Word of God with practical Christian living stressed.	Emphasis on Word and sacrament with call to make faith active in love.
Statistics*	Membership . . . . 2,494,574 Congregations . . . . 11,920 *Statistics from the Assemblies of God.	

CHAPTER 3

Baptist Church

The name *Baptist* denotes one of the chief characteristics of Baptists—their doctrine of baptism. Baptists accept believer's baptism but reject infant baptism. They were originally led to this doctrine of baptism by their study of the New Testament where they found instances of believer's baptism but failed to find any instances of infant baptism. (There is, however, a good possibility that baptisms of households, as in Acts 16:33, included infants.)

Baptists are known for baptizing adult believers by immersion.

Baptist Beginnings

There is no agreement among Baptist historians regarding Baptist beginnings. Some of the older historians believed that Baptists began with John the Baptist and repeatedly reemerged as various sects within the church. Other historians regard these groups as forerunners of Baptists and believe that Baptists really began among Separatists from the Church of England who were influenced by Dutch Mennonites in the early seventeenth century.

What seems beyond doubt is that during the Reformation of the sixteenth century two contrasting views emerged. One was *reformation:* the view of Luther, Zwingli, Calvin, and the reformers of the church in England. The other was *restitution:* the restoration of the first-century church as depicted in the New Testament. This was the view of the Anabaptists, such as Grebel, Blaurock, Hübmaier, and Manz.

Although the first Anabaptists—so named by their opponents, who regarded them as re- *(ana)* baptizers—were baptized as infants, they also baptized one another as believers. By this action they separated themselves from the other churches of the Reformation era to form so-called pure churches, that is, churches consisting of Christian believers who had undergone believer's baptism. But just as there were various kinds of Lutherans, so there were various kind of Anabaptists. At the one extreme were the militant Anabaptists of the city of Münster in Germany, who in 1534 tried to restore the "pure church" by violence. At the other extreme were the mild Anabaptists, such as Menno Simons of

Holland, who founded the Mennonites. It was a group of these Dutch Mennonites, the Waterlander Mennonites, that eventually strongly influenced the group that became the first English Baptists.

In its early history, the Church of England was torn between factions favorable to the Roman Catholic Church and those who wanted to split from Rome. Queen Elizabeth I resolved to end this pendulum movement by establishing a church of the "middle way" between Protestantism and Catholicism. But this middle way did not satisfy everybody. Some extreme Protestants began to separate from the Church of England. These Separatist groups were often persecuted, and in 1608 one such group, led by John Smyth, emigrated to Amsterdam, Holland. There they were influenced by the Waterlander Mennonites to reject infant baptism and practice only believer's baptism. Smyth then baptized himself and other members of his group. He became a Mennonite and died in Holland. Other members of his group declined to become Mennonites, and in 1612, led by Thomas Helwys, they returned to England to form the first Baptist church on English soil at Spitalfields near London.

These earliest English Baptists were Arminian in theology; that is, they believed that God desires to save all people and that salvation depends on both divine grace and human free will. They further believed that each local church should be independent of church authority and state authority. The English Baptists formed voluntary associations of churches for mutual help and became known as General Baptists.

Other Baptists, however, accepted the Calvinistic idea that God predetermines that certain people shall be saved and others lost. These Calvinistic Baptists became known as Particular Baptists.

Baptists in the United States

The earliest Baptists in the United States came from England to New England and from there spread throughout the states.

In 1630 Roger Williams, not yet a Baptist but a devotee of religious liberty, fled to Massachusetts to escape persecution in England. However, Williams was similarly forced to flee from there to the Indian territory surrounding Massachusetts, where he founded the city of Providence and the state of Rhode Island. He was able to obtain a charter for the new state that guaranteed religious liberty. From Rhode Island, Baptists gradually spread throughout the United States, forming associations as in England.

Like other Protestant denominations, Baptists became divided by the tensions of the Civil War period. Already in 1845 Baptists in the southern states founded the Southern Baptist Convention. Baptists in the northern states, while maintaining local associations, were slower to unite into a convention. In 1907, however, they formed the Northern Baptist Convention, which was later renamed the American Baptist Convention, and later still the American Baptist Churches. Since that time, there have been other, smaller divisions.

A large number of African Americans were attracted to the Baptist Church, but they were not welcomed into the white churches or conventions. They formed their own conventions, such as the National Baptist Convention, the National Convention, Inc., and the Progressive Baptist Convention. There has been some progress at integrating the Baptist bodies, and some black churches have fairly close relations with the American Baptist Churches.

Basic Baptist Principles

Despite their differences and divisions, most Baptists have throughout their history held four principles in common:

- the restitution or restoration of the New Testament church in later times, including our own; the restitution, that is, of a regenerate church membership;
- the practice of believer's baptism only, without infant baptism, as a means of restoring the New Testament church and keeping it pure;
- a congregational church structure in which each member has a vote, and each local church is independent of the others, though free to enter into association with others while maintaining its autonomy;
- a commitment to defending religious freedom at all levels including the freedom of the local church within the denomination, the freedom of each denomination to make its own decisions without pressure from any other denomination, and the freedom of each local congregation and of each denomination from the state.

In addition to these four principles, two others may be mentioned as defining Baptist belief, particularly in the Southern Baptist Convention:

- a reliance on the New Testament teaching of the priesthood of all believers, whereby all Christians have direct access to God, not mediated by a separate structure of clergy;
- an insistence on Scripture, often interpreted quite literally, as providing the sole authority for teaching and belief.

Baptist Theology

Basic Baptist principles are clear, but Baptist theology is extremely varied. This is due in part to the constant Baptist stress on religious freedom and in part to Baptist neglect of creeds and confessions of faith.

Unlike most Christian denominations, Baptists in general do not use the ancient Christian creeds either in worship or in Christian education. They see themselves as confessional (in a broad sense) rather than creedal. However, Baptists have from time to time adopted statements of belief, as for instance when the Southern Baptists have reaffirmed and clarified the Baptist Faith and Message.

Like most other Protestant denominations, Baptists understand the authority of the Bible in different ways. Baptist fundamentalists believe that the Bible is directly the Word of God and therefore inerrant. Other Baptists, however, believe that the Bible is the Word of God mediated through the word of human beings—prophets, psalmists, historians, apostles, and evangelists—and therefore not inerrant.

Baptists retain two ordinances, baptism and the Lord's supper. Baptists insist that the practice of baptism be restricted to those persons who already have faith in Christ. Believer's baptism is understood by most Baptists to be a *sign* of salvation, not a *means* of salvation. Baptists also practice the Lord's supper, generally following the understanding that the supper is a memorial meal only and not a means of grace.

Baptist and Ecumenism

Baptists participate in ecumenism in varying degrees. Some are deeply concerned about peace and justice in the world; others have little interest in this. Some are concerned with interreligious dialogue and are willing to learn from other religions; others are not. On the question of Christian unity, some Baptists would reject any dialogue, collaboration, or union with other denominations, regarding them as false churches; others would allow for dialogue or collaboration (seeing some degree of validity in the other denominations), but still refuse union; and a few Baptist churches favor participation in organizations such as the Consultation on Church Union together with a reconsideration and possible modification of the traditional basic Baptist principles.

For Discussion

□ What do the different teachings about Baptism (infant versus believer's) say about how God is at work in the person?
□ How important do you think it is that the present-day church be closely modeled on the first-century church?
□ In what ways do you think Baptists might define *unity of the church* differently from Lutherans? Think, for instance, of the use or nonuse of creeds.

For Further Study

□ *The Baptists* by Anne Devereaux Jordan and J. M. Stifle (New York: Hippocrene Books, 1990)
□ *Baptist Battles: Social Change and Religious Conflict in the Southern Baptist Convention* by Nancy Tatom Ammerman (New Brunswick: Rutgers University Press, 1990)
□ Southern Baptist Convention web site: www.sbcnet.org

Table of Comparison	*Baptists*	*Lutherans*
Teachings	1. Accept the Bible as Word of God. Some conservative Baptists very literal in interpretation. 2. Accept no creeds, with each person to interpret Bible for him- or herself. Baptists refuse to use creeds as a "test of faith." 3. Practice only "believer's Baptism." 4. Believe immersion is the only scriptural method of Baptism. 5. Practice two ordinances: baptism and Lord's supper. Communion considered a sign of salvation.	1. Accept the Bible as the written witness to God's revelation of saving action through Jesus Christ. 2. Accept the historic creeds as definitions and summaries of biblical truth. 3. Baptize both infants and adults. 4. Stress baptism by water in the name of the Father, Son, and Holy Spirit, regardless of method (submersion, immersion, or pouring). 5. Practice two sacraments: Baptism and Holy Communion as God's means of conveying God's grace.
Type of Worship	Free and generally unstructured, according to choice of congregation and minister.	Liturgical pattern based on tradition of the Western church.
Government	Congregational form regarded as only scriptural type. Some joint work through Conventions.	Interdependent congregational, regional, national, and global expressions of the church characterized by democratic decision making, strong ecumenical relationships, elected leadership, and an ordained ministry.
Characteristics	Stress placed on personal conversion, sometimes with accompanying emotional experience. Strongly opposed to mixture of church and state.	Emphasize God's action of grace in receiving people through Baptism and in strengthening them through Word and Communion. Affirm separation of church and state.
Statistics*	Membership ....34,691,179 Congregations ....89,713 *U. S. statistics of 12 Baptist denominations from *Yearbook of American and Canadian Churches 1998*.	

CHAPTER 4

Buddhism

Buddhism features many forms of meditation. All forms of meditation seek ultimately to allow the practitioner to let go of his or her ego.

Trying to describe Buddhism is a little like trying to describe a snowflake—or Christianity. Buddhism has taken many forms in its 2,500-year history. Some forms of Buddhism are nontheistic, while the adherents of other forms pray to various "gods." Some emphasize meditation while others argue that only faith matters. This proliferation of forms—schools, branches, sects—has been the result of Buddhism's inclusiveness and openness, which led to a tendency to absorb local cultures and religious forms, as it spread outward from India to Southeast Asia, China, Korea, Japan, and Tibet. This adaptability has made Buddhism enormously successful; more than 50 percent of the world's population live in areas where Buddhism has been the dominant religious force at some time. Despite repression in Communist countries, it is still the major religion in most of Asia. Among this proliferation of branches, however, all forms of Buddhism have the same root: the life and teachings of Gautama (or Gotama) Buddha.

The Historical Buddha

The term *Buddha* is a title that means "one who has been awakened" or "the Enlightened One." Although it might be applied to any wise being (in Buddhism there are both incarnated and nonincarnated or "celestial" Buddhas), it has been traditionally reserved for that rare individual who has a transcendent and transformative insight into the nature of reality. Any person has the potential to become a Buddha, though the title has usually been used to refer to the historical Buddha, Gautama Buddha.

Gautama Buddha was born as Siddhartha, a prince of the Sakya clan, in what is now Nepal near its border with India. Although the dates are controversial, most scholars think Siddhartha was born around 566 B.C.E. Siddhartha's father belonged to a warrior caste and was a governor of the area in which he lived, so Siddhartha was raised in comfort. As time passed, he grew up, married, and had a son. At the age of 29, he left home and family to start a spiritual quest to understand the suffering he saw around him. He studied with religious teachers and learned ascetic practices that he followed strictly for six years. He finally realized, however, that these practices were not leading him closer to enlightenment, so he abandoned them. Alone, meditating under a Bodhi tree, he reached enlightenment at the age of 35. Siddhartha, now *Sakyamuni* (meaning "the Sage of the Sakya clan") or Gautama Buddha, went to Benares, India, where he preached his first sermon. He devoted the next 45 years to wandering and preaching in northern India, spending the rainy season (June–September) in a monastery. He attracted many disciples, both lay and monastic, men and women. He died a peaceful and natural death at 80 years.

The Heart of the Buddha's Teaching

At the core of all forms of Buddhism are the Four Noble Truths and the Eight-fold Path, the heart of Gautama's insights into reality and especially the human condition.

The first Noble Truth is that *life is suffering*. This does not mean that there are no moments of happiness, but that these moments are not permanent. Even the most fortunate of us inevitably experiences disappointment.

The second Noble Truth is that *there is a reason for this suffering*. Suffering obviously may be caused by painful events—not getting the job we wanted or losing a friend, for instance—but these events caused suffering because of our underlying desire and attachment. We suffer because we can't always get what we want. We suffer when we lose a person to whom we were attached. Because of this attachment, in fact, suffering is inevitable because life is change. There is no way to prolong life, much less happy moments, indefinitely.

But isn't it human nature to desire and to become attached to things and to people? Of course! Does this mean that suffering is inevitable and that we just need to accept it? Here, the Buddha's answer was no. The third Noble Truth is that *there is a way to end suffering*, and the fourth Noble Truth is that *the way to end suffering is the Eight-fold Path*.

The Eight-fold Path can be arranged under three headings: wisdom, morality, and concentration.

Wisdom

- *Right Views*—understanding the Buddha's teachings and Truth/Reality.
- *Right Aspirations*—high and noble aims.

Morality

- *Right Speech*—speaking kind words and truth; not lying, gossiping, being verbally abusive.
- *Right Conduct*—good, moral, compassionate behavior.
- *Right Livelihood*—having an honest living that does not cause suffering to others.

Concentration

- *Right Effort*—perseverance in goodness and clearing the mind.
- *Right Mindfulness*—attentiveness to reality and the present moment.
- *Right Meditation*—concentration on Buddha and the *Dharma* (Buddha's teachings and the basic truth of things), using meditation as an instrument to attain enlightenment.

Like the Ten Commandments, one needs to practice all of the Eight-fold Path simultaneously; there is no necessary progression. There seems to be a logical order, though, in that the first two "steps" have to do with coming to understand the Buddha's teachings and wanting to improve one's life; the next three have to do with moral action in everyday life; and the last three have to do with practices that deepen understanding of life and reality. However, one can practice Right Conduct, for instance, without understanding Buddha's teachings or meditating.

Clearly, though, the practices reinforce and deepen each other. Following the Eight-fold Path leads to Nirvana, the cessation of suffering. Although Nirvana is sometimes depicted as a place (comparable to heaven) in paintings and literature, it can also be seen as the state of highest consciousness, a perfect understanding of reality. Rejecting the extreme ascetic practices then in use, Buddha taught a "way of moderation," "a middle way," placing enlightenment and salvation from suffering within reach of ordinary people as well as monastic followers.

Other Principal Buddhist Concepts

Buddha-nature and Boddhisattvas. Buddhism teaches that all people have a Buddha-nature, a spark of the Divine; however, most of us have a hard time getting in touch with and expressing that spark because our ego and desires distort our vision of reality and our ability to respond to others purely and altruistically. The various practices taught to reach enlightenment are aimed at erasing the ego and attachment in order to help us see reality more clearly and get in touch with that spark of the Divine. It is like dispelling the clouds covering the sun. Enlightenment, a transcendent understanding of reality, leads naturally to wisdom and compassion. The ideal person, especially in Mahayana Buddhism, is the *Boddhisattva,* one who reaches enlightenment but remains in human form to teach and lead others to Nirvana. Boddhisattva, like Buddha, is a title. Thus, Jesus, for instance, could be considered a boddhisattva.

Karma. *Karma* is the law of cause and effect, as you sow so shall you reap. But what about those people who seem to get away with evil deeds? Some forms of Buddhism believe in reincarnation, so deeds done in this life may affect future lives even when the law of karma seems not to have "worked" in the short run. These Buddhists believe one is especially lucky to be born human because it is in this form that one has the most freedom to create (and improve) one's destiny. But on a psychological level, the law of karma is always operating in that our actions affect who we are—by doing good things, we become better persons.

Meditation and Egolessness. Many forms of Buddhism teach various forms of meditation with perhaps seemingly different goals—emptying or focusing the mind or sending lovingkindness, for instance. However, at base, all forms of meditation seek ultimately to allow the practitioner to rise above or let go of his or her ego. Have you ever had an experience where you were so caught up in something that you didn't notice the time passing? This is a glimpse of the experience of egolessness. *No self* does not mean having no personality, but being released from the anxieties and distortions caused by the ego, which limits us, to see reality more clearly and to go with the flow of the moment more purely, to be a better conduit for the boundless love and energy of the universe. Meditation and especially the idea of no-self or egolessness as a goal seems to be strange to many Americans who often make heroes of the individual. Really, though, how different is this from Jesus saying "whoever wants to be first must be last of all and servant of all," or his prayer "not my will but yours be done"?

Mindfulness. Meditation is also practice in *mindfulness,* paying attention to the present moment. Every moment presents the opportunity to see reality more deeply and clearly, but most of the time we are too preoccupied by our own concerns to pay attention to what is *really* around us. However, meditation is not emphasized in all Buddhist schools because Buddhists believe that any act—sweeping the floor or washing the dishes—can be a sacred act, a path toward enlightenment if done mindfully. The Buddha avoided the dogmatism of his age, and Buddhism generally teaches that specific religious practices are not important as long as the aims are not lost.

Development of Buddhism

Before his death, the Buddha is reported to have told his followers that thereafter the *Dharma* (that is, "the Teachings") would be their teacher. These teachings are contained in the *Tripitakas* (translated "the Three Baskets"). The Sutra Pitaka contains the addresses and sermons for the laity. The Vinaya Pitaka contains the rules of conduct for the monks and their communities. The Abhidharma Pitaka was a later development (starting c. 350 B.C.E.) containing the metaphysics and philosophy of Buddhism in a more systematic fashion. These teachings were originally handed down orally with more attention paid to their content than actual words. Disciples were allowed to recite the scriptures in their own dialects. Versions of the canon exist in Sanskrit, Pali, Chinese, Japanese, and Tibetan, reflecting not only its Indian origins (the Sanskrit and Pali texts) but also its transmission to other Asian countries.

Buddhism got a tremendous boost by its enthusiastic adoption in the third century B.C.E. by King Ashoka in India. Ashoka had authority over a great part of southern Asia and sent many missionaries. By the first century C.E., Buddhism was a powerful force in India and Sri Lanka (Ceylon). From these roots, Buddhism was introduced by trade routes to Southeast Asia, China (first century), Korea (fourth century), Japan (sixth century), and Tibet (seventh century). Buddhism was so successful because its openness allowed it to assimilate local cultural and religious practices. Also, different sects could emphasize different elements in the teachings; however, most forms of Buddhism can be associated with one of three main branches: Hinayana (Southern), Mahayana (Eastern), and Tantric (Northern) Buddhism.

Hinayana Buddhism consists of the sects that emphasize the attainment of enlightenment through self-power, following the example of Gautama Buddha. This form of Buddhism is the oldest and most conservative form of Buddhism and is more prevalent in India, Sri Lanka, and Southeast Asia (Burma, Cambodia, Laos, and Thailand). Mahayana Buddhism arose in the second century after the death of Buddha, splitting from the Hinayana schools, and emphasizes the need for help from another power and the potential for anyone to become a boddhisattva. This more liberal form of Buddhism is prevalent in China, Korea, Japan, Vietnam, Tibet, and Mongolia. Tantric Buddhism emphasizes more mystical and magical elements such as the use of mandalas and mantras. Tantric forms of Buddhism coexist with others schools of Buddhism, perhaps most notably in Tibet.

Buddhism Comes to America

Although Buddhism spread throughout Asia, it was slow to come to the West. Buddhist (and Hindu) ideas were introduced through transcendentalist writers like Ralph Waldo Emerson and Henry David Thoreau as well as Theosophists in the nineteenth century, but knowledge of Buddhism was sketchy and imperfect. Buddhism as a religion came to America with the Chinese immigrants who worked on the railroads and in the gold fields of the West in the mid-nineteenth century. Buddhism was further strengthened with the Japanese immigration to Hawaii and the West Coast at the turn of the century. This immigration led to the founding of ethnic Buddhist temples. The first Buddhist temple in the United States was the First Chinese Buddhist Temple, founded in San Francisco in 1853. The Japanese community started the Buddhist Mission of North America (which became the Buddhist Churches of America) in San Francisco in 1899.

From the late nineteenth century on, Buddhism gradually achieved a wider American audience. Japanese teachers brought Zen Buddhism, a sect of the Mahayana branch, to this country, and it became especially widely known in the 1950s and 1960s when Beat and counterculture writers took it up. The late 1960s saw the establishment of groups founded by Tibetan Buddhists led by charismatic leaders, most notably at the Nyingmapa Center in Berkeley, California, and the Naropa Institute originally in Vermont but now in Boulder, Colorado. The 1970s saw a revived interest in another sect known as Theravada Buddhism but with a new emphasis on meditation as reflected in the establishment of the Insight Meditation Center in Vermont to teach *Vipassana* (lovingkindness) meditation.

Buddhism in America: Zen and Shin Buddhism

When Americans think of Buddhism, the images that generally come to mind are monks in orange robes from Southeast Asia or Tibet or people doing Zen meditation. The former image springs from our TV viewing and knowledge of world affairs, the latter from the tremendous popularity of Zen among Americans.

Zen's popularity in America was helped by its adoption by the Beats in the 1950s and the counterculture in the 1960s. Writers such as Allen Ginsberg, Jack Kerouac, Gary Snyder, and Robert Pirsig helped increased Zen's visibility. One of the important elements to notice here is that all of these writers are white. White American Buddhists tend to follow one of three traditions—Zen, Tibetan, or Vipassana Buddhism. All of these sects emphasize meditation as the path to enlightenment, with the result that many Americans mistakenly equate Buddhism with meditation. The emphasis that these sects place on self-reliance, on "virtuoso" spiritual practices (long meditation retreats, for instance), and on enlightenment as a goal, all appeal to competitive and individualistic America—particularly the highly educated, middle to upper class white Americans who are most attracted to these forms of Buddhism.

By contrast, the other most prevalent form of Buddhism in America is almost invisible: Shin Buddhism, often considered the "protestant" wing of Buddhism because of its emphasis that the key to Nirvana is faith rather than any rigorous ritual or strict ascetic practice. Shin Buddhism is little known because it is almost totally an ethnic religion brought by Japanese immigrants (mostly poor farmers) at the turn of the century. Discouraged from assimilation in the first half of this century by prejudice and discrimination, first-generation Japanese Americans nurtured Japanese culture and values in their children through the Buddhist temple. But farsighted early church leaders also encouraged Americanization, blending East and West by adapting hymns, developing Sunday school programs, and organizing Boy Scout troops. The Buddhist Churches of America is now almost 100 years old and nationwide; however, because Shin Buddhism has remained mainly an ethnic church, the numbers have been decreasing as more and more Japanese Americans marry out.

Buddhism in America has been growing steadily in the second half of the twentieth century. There are many reasons for this, including the increased interest in spirituality in general in our very materialistic and secularized society; however, some of the reasons can be found within Buddhism itself. The goal of enlightenment, the idea of karma, and the Buddha's encouragement to test the teachings of the Buddha against one's experience and not rely on tradition, dogma, or authority parallel America's generally experiential and scientific worldview. The Buddha did not concern himself with questions such as who created the universe, but focused only on what he felt was essential for spiritual development. This focus on the practical also perhaps appeals to our more skeptical age. Furthermore, Buddhism's philosophical and psychological understanding and sophistication match our own.

Despite repression in many Communist countries, Buddhism remains a vital force in the world today, especially in Asia but increasingly in North America. After 2,500 years, the Buddha's teachings also remain as profound and relevant as ever. Buddhism has much to offer to people of all faiths in understanding the human condition and the causes and cures of suffering.

For Discussion

□ What aspects of Buddhism are attractive to you, and why?
□ Generally speaking, Buddhism is inclusive of other faiths, while Christianity historically has presented itself as the only way to salvation. What factors may have contributed to these different approaches?
□ Though it is an ancient religion, Buddhism was slow to catch on in the West, yet now it is attracting many followers here. Why do you think this is so?

For Further Study

□ Any book by Vietnamese Buddhist monk Thich Nhat Hanh; especially interesting to Christians might be *Living Buddha, Living Christ.*
□ *Shambala: The Way of the Warrior* by Chogyam Trungpa
□ *Zen Mind, Beginner's Mind* by Shinryu Suzuki, ed. Trudy Dixon
□ *Shinran's Gospel of Pure Grace* by Alfred Bloom

Table of Comparison	*Buddhism*	*Lutherans*
Teachings	1. "God" understood as ultimate reality, the All. Not concerned with how universe was created. 2. The goal of Buddhism is enlightenment (perfect understanding of reality, which leads to compassion for all beings) and Nirvana (cessation of suffering). 3. Buddhists believe the Four Noble Truths and the Eight-fold Path but are encouraged to test teachings against their own experience. 4. All people have a Buddha-nature, the potential to become a Buddha or Boddhisattva (like Gautama Buddha or Jesus). 5. Buddhists believe in karma, the law of cause and effect. Many Buddhists believe in reincarnation.	1. Believe in personal, triune God—Father (Creator), Son (Redeemer), Holy Spirit (Sanctifier). 2. Christian life is directed toward salvation through God's grace and love for God and people. 3. God's will is revealed in the scriptures in Law and Gospel; though interpreted in everyday living, these teachings are unchanging. 4. Jesus was the unique Son of God; we are encouraged to imitate his faithfulness, but must rely on his death for our salvation. 5. Though humans have freedom to disobey God and their actions have effects, all is under the umbrella of God's law and grace. Each human has one earthly life.
Type of Worship	Varies according to sect. Most common elements are chanting, an incense offering, silent meditation, and a talk by a priest or monk.	Liturgical from tradition with basic order followed by custom and church statements.
Government	Varies. Some Buddhist sects are directed by teachers, others are less hierarchical.	Interdependent congregational, regional, national, and global expressions of the church characterized by democratic decision making, strong ecumenical relationships, elected leadership, and an ordained ministry.
Characteristics	Strongest among Asian Americans, with increasing appeal among non-Asian middle and upper classes.	Strongest appeal among the middle class, although not exclusively so.
Statistics*	Est. North American membership . . . 2,132,000 U. S. membership, Buddhist Churches of America . . . . 780,000 Congregations, BCA . . . . 199 **1998 Encyclopædia Britannica Book of the Year.*	

CHAPTER 5

The Christian and Missionary Alliance

Hymn singing is an important part of the free and informal worship services in Alliance churches.

The Christian and Missionary Alliance was founded by Dr. Albert B. Simpson, a Presbyterian minister who in 1881 felt called to evangelize the masses of New York City and to send missionaries to preach the gospel in foreign lands.

In 1887 Dr. Simpson organized an interdenominational fellowship called The Christian Alliance and an international missionary society called The Evangelical Missionary Alliance. These two were combined in 1897 as The Christian and Missionary Alliance.

At the present time, the Alliance sponsors more than 1,100 overseas missionaries who are serving in 46 mission fields located in Asia, Africa, South America, and the Middle East, as well as special ministries in Europe. This vast missionary program is supported mainly by the 2,350 Alliance churches in the United States and Canada.

The Alliance World Fellowship, of which the Christian and Missionary Alliance in the United States is a member, has 15,000 churches and 2.4 million members in 61 nations and territories. The AWF is a consultative organization that sponsors international missions projects and meets quadrennially for mutual exchange of information and encouragement.

The Alliance is evangelical and conservative in its theology and adheres to the traditional orthodox position of the Christian church. Above all, it is Christ-centered. This is reflected in the use of the term *The Fourfold Gospel* which means: Christ, our Savior; Christ, our Sanctifier; Christ, our Healer; and Christ, our Coming King.

It is affirmed that the Old and New Testaments, inerrant as originally given, were verbally inspired by God and are a complete revelation of God's will for the salvation of humankind. The scriptures constitute the divine and only rule of Christian faith and practice.

Alliance churches conduct free and informal worship services that include hymn singing, prayer, and the reading of the scriptures. A prominent place is always given to the preaching of the Word. Two ordinances are practiced: baptism and the Lord's supper. Baptism is only used for adults and young people as a testimony of their faith.

For Discussion

□ Reflecting its name, the Christian and Missionary Alliance places a large emphasis on foreign missions. What do you know about your own church's mission outreach? How does it compare?

□ Look at The Fourfold Gospel above. Which of these titles for Christ do you think your church would stress the most?

□ Compare the Alliance's understanding of baptism with that of your church.

For Further Study

□ *All for Jesus,* a centennial history of the Christian and Missionary Alliance, by Robert L. Niklaus (Camp Hill, Penn.: Christian Publications, 1996)

□ The Christian and Missionary Alliance Web site: www.cmalliance.org

Table of Comparison	*The Christian and Missionary Alliance*	*Lutherans*
Teachings	1. Believe in the inerrancy of the Scriptures as originally given. 2. Affirm the triune nature of God. 3. Accept Jesus Christ as truly divine and human. 4. Practice two ordinances: baptism for converted adults by immersion and the Lord's supper. 5. Church comprised of believers redeemed through the blood of Christ. It is commissioned to preach the gospel to all nations.	1. Accept the Bible as the written witness to God's revelation of saving action through Jesus Christ. 2. Same. 3. Same. 4. Sacraments of Baptism and the Lord's Supper are channels of God's grace for God's people. 5. Church is the body of Christ and exists where God's Word is preached and the sacraments are rightly administered.
Type of Worship	Free and informal. Nonliturgical with hymn singing, prayers, and scripture reading. Sermon given prominent place.	Liturgical following the tradition of the Western church. Both Word and sacrament considered important.
Government	Resembles presbyterian form, with elders, deacons, and trustees in local congregation. Have District Conferences and annual General Council.	Interdependent congregational, regional, national, and global expressions of the church characterized by democratic decision making, strong ecumenical relationships, elected leadership, and an ordained ministry.
Characteristics	Major emphasis on world missions, with a considerable number of missionaries.	World missions considered a part of the church's total ministry.
Statistics*	Membership . . . . 328,000 Congregations . . . . 1,964 *from The Christian and Missionary Alliance.	

CHAPTER 6

Christian Church (Disciples of Christ)

Thomas Campbell, an early leader of the Christian Church, traveled on horseback to preach in homes and in outdoor settings.

The Christian Church (Disciples of Christ) is one of the younger church bodies in the world and is typically American in its origin and outlook. It had its beginning on the frontier in the early nineteenth century, growing out of a desire for freedom from religious traditions and an impulse for Christian unity.

The primary witness of this body of people is for the unity of Christ's church. There is, however, a basic difference of opinion on how this goal is to be reached. The congregations and members related to the General Assembly of the Christian Church in the United States and Canada see the fulfillment of this goal coming through work in the National and World Councils of Churches, dialogue with the Consultation on Church Union (COCU), and support of similar movements. Other independent Christian Churches, not related to the General Assembly, envision unity as the outcome of other religious denominations conforming to what the independent Christian Churches consider to be the pattern of the New Testament church.

Freedom and unity are themes that flow through the entire history of the Christian Church (Disciples of Christ). An early leader was Thomas Campbell (1763–1854), a Seceder Presbyterian minister who came to the United States from Ireland in 1807 and was assigned a parish in western Pennsylvania. His parish was a long circuit that had to be traveled on horseback. People who came to him were not all of the same branch of Presbyterianism, yet to him, they were all one people needing his ministry. The synod did not see his responsibility in this way, and he was soon a minister without a parish.

Disciples of Christ

In reaction to his dismissal, Thomas Campbell began a reform program emphasizing the need for Christian unity based on the Word of God. Soon the Christian Association of Washington, Pennsylvania, was formed. This organization was simply a community of persons concerned with finding ways and means of achieving the union of existing churches. The Disciples of Christ developed out of this movement.

When the Christian Association needed a rationale, Thomas Campbell prepared a 56-page document called the *Declaration and Address of the Christian Association of Washington*. It was adopted by the Association's members in 1809 and is now one of the basic historical documents of the Christian Church (Disciples of Christ).

In the meantime Alexander Campbell (1788–1866), son of Thomas Campbell, arrived in America with his father's family. Even before learning of his father's estrangement with the Presbyterians, young Campbell had become an independent in his religious views and an advocate of Christian unity. He readily accepted the principles of the *Declaration and Address* and determined to devote his life to them.

Brush Run and Beyond

The members of the Association thought they could best witness to Christian unity not by fighting within established denominations but by forming a separate congregation. The Christian Association was constituted as the Brush Run Church in 1811. Alexander Campbell was chosen as its minister. A few years later, the Association became affiliated with the Mahoning Baptist Association in Ohio.

A journal called *The Christian Baptist,* edited by Campbell, had a tremendous influence on the American frontier. It carried on a crusade against authoritarian creeds, the professional clergy, missionary societies, and ecclesiasticism. It spoke also on the positive side by advocating a restoration of apostolic Christianity as a solid basis on which all churches could unite. This was the task of a *new* reformation.

Soon there were reformers in many Baptist congregations. Some of these churches remained loyal to Baptist tradition, a few divided, and still others dissolved as Baptist bodies to embrace the new movement of unity.

Christian Churches

Even before Campbell started to work among the Baptists there were other expressions of the freedom movement in American church life in the early nineteenth century. Elias Smith and Abner Jones established what they called Christian Churches in New England. Also, a minister named James O'Kelly broke with the Methodists over the matter of ecclesiastical authority. With several other ministers he withdrew from Methodist jurisdiction and formed the Republican Methodist Church. This group, prominent in North Carolina, Virginia, and Kentucky, soon adopted the name Christian Church.

The strongest Christian Church group, however, was one that originated in Kentucky under the leadership of Barton W. Stone. He was a Presbyterian minister who had participated in the great revival at Cane Ridge, Kentucky, working with ministers of many faiths. For this, he and others were censured by the Synod of Kentucky. This led them to renounce the jurisdiction of the Synod and form independent and "free" Christian churches.

These various Christian Church groups, since they were advocating the same principles—freedom, Christian unity, and congregational autonomy—discovered one another and joined forces. They objected to formal creeds as being divisive, ecclesiasticism as being oppressive, and advocated liberty and Christian unity.

The views of these groups were similar to those of the Baptist reformers, the Disciples of Christ group. Differences between the two movements were more a matter of emphasis than of doctrine. The "reformers" placed restoration of early Christianity and church unity first; the "Christians" stressed liberty and freedom as being first.

Unions Church by Church

It was inevitable that the Baptist reformers and the Christians would become one people. In the 1830s the two bodies united, both at a leadership level and church by church. The reformers preferred the name "Disciples of Christ" for the total group. The "Christians" could not give up their original name. Because agreement has not been possible, the corporate name, Christian Church (Disciples of Christ) is used today. (There were some Christian Churches who remained separate until 1931 when they became a part of what is now the United Church of Christ.)

Theological Approach: Bible for Creeds

Until recent times there was little interest in theology as such. In general the churches followed the view of Alexander Campbell who said, "Let the Bible be substituted for all human creeds." Since they were advocating simple evangelical Christianity, members of these churches had no interest in analyzing the nature of God, though they affirmed belief in God the Father, Son, and Holy Spirit.

On theological issues such as sin and salvation, the divinity of Christ, the virgin birth, the bodily resurrection, and the second coming of the Lord there is no more divergence of views than can be found within any other one recognized denomination. The profession of faith in the terms of Peter's confession (Matthew 16:16) and the Reformation principle of the priesthood of all believers are accepted doctrine in the Christian Church.

Although Christian Church members usually take a cautious and guarded stance toward tradition and creeds, a very open position is assumed on the Bible. They look at the Bible for answers to theological questions. The gospel proclamation and the need for the person to respond are emphasized.

Because of its witness for Christian unity, the main emphasis of this religious body has been in the visible church. There has always been an interest in the structure and activity of the church, but the emphasis has been on the fellowship. At the same time, the church has never been considered as a moral society only, but as a divine institution. The *ecclesia* is both the local church and the church universal.

Two Ordinances

Christian Churches observe two sacraments (called ordinances): the Lord's supper and baptism. The first ordinance is celebrated each Sunday as the center of corporate worship. The second ordinance is administered to believers only and by immersion. Some of the more liberal congregations will accept the baptismal experience of persons coming from a denomination where another form of baptism is practiced.

The Lord's supper is thought to be a memorial, as fellowship with Christ and as a channel of God's grace. It is administered by the minister and two laypersons (called Elders) who have been selected by the congregation, and distributed by several other selected laypersons (called Deacons). Participation is open to all persons regardless of denomination. Eligibility is on the basis of the individual conscience with Paul's admonition (1 Corinthians 11:27-29) in mind.

Ministry and Worship

Though the historical doctrine of apostolic succession is rejected as being a stumbling block to Christian unity, it is the belief of these people that the apostolic church did set apart certain people for its ministry and that the church has this responsibility today. Therefore, the Christian Church is concerned with theological education, not on a denominational basis, but on a broad ecumenical basis that includes various special ministries. The minister is looked upon, in the Christian Church, as the spiritual and administrative leader of the congregation.

Worship practice in this denomination is not confined to any specific liturgical form. Each congregation is free to develop its own; on occasion ancient liturgies are used, but the minister has the privilege of being creative at this point to make public worship relevant to the times and to special situations.

Social Issues

Since congregations are autonomous units, agreement on social issues is obtained by exchange of opinion. The General Assembly regularly formulates its views on matters of social import, but only as a recommendation and not as legislation. The Division of Homeland Ministries and other general administrative units of the church offer program guidance and provide social issues resources for the congregations. Peace with justice is a General Assembly-approved priority. This priority is expressed through refugee resettlement efforts, ecumenical service projects, and the giving of material aid. Christian Churches also identify with the social ministries of the councils of churches, regional, national, and world. Representatives are sent to all ecumenical conferences and Christian churches are sensitive to the Christian social consciences of other denominations.

Affirming the unity of Christians as their polar star, the Christian churches resolve, "Where the Scriptures speak, we speak; where the Scriptures are silent, we are silent."

For Discussion

□ Why do you think Disciples and Lutherans have such different views regarding the historic structures of the church?
□ Compare attitudes toward church union of the Christian Church and the Lutheran church.
□ Do you think it is appropriate for the church to speak, for instance, on social issues where "the Scriptures are silent"? Why or why not?

For Further Study

□ *The Faith We Affirm: Basic Beliefs of Disciples of Christ* by Ronald E. Osborn (Chalice Press, 1986)
□ *Disciples at Prayer: The Spirituality of the Christian Church (Disciples of Christ)* by William O. Paulsell (Chalice Press, 1996)
□ Christian Church (Disciples of Christ) Web site: www.disciples.org

Table of Comparison	*Christian Church (Disciples of Christ)*	*Lutherans*
Teachings	1. Human statements of faith used for insight but are not binding or authoritative. 2. A person's duty to become a Christian involves confession of Jesus as Christ, repentance, and baptism. 3. Original sin denied, but the person with free will is accountable to God. 4. Holy Communion observed in fellowship as a memorial to Christ and as a channel of God's grace. 5. Advocate Christian unity; believe division in Christ's church is sin.	1. Creeds, catechisms, and confessions used as summaries of scripture's teachings. 2. God's gospel proclaimed for humankind's response of faith by the power of the Holy Spirit. 3. Original sin seen as the condition of human nature in need of grace. 4. Holy Communion is the celebration of Christ's real presence and is a means of grace. 5. Increasingly accepting of fellowship with similar Christian denominations.
Type of Worship	Free to use traditional forms of liturgy or to create forms relevant to times and specific situations. Communion celebrated each Lord's Day as focal point of worship.	Liturgical order utilized with Eucharist celebrated with increasing frequency in realizing the unity of Word and sacrament.
Government	Local church autonomy; cooperation with other Christian churches in missionary and benevolent work; hold International Convention; support ecumenical structures.	Interdependent congregational, regional, national, and global expressions of the church characterized by democratic decision making, strong ecumenical relationships, elected leadership, and an ordained ministry.
Characteristics	Strong emphasis on Bible; priesthood of all believers; members admitted when they reach age of accountability, make public statement of faith, and receive baptism; witness to Christian unity.	Strong emphasis is on Word and sacrament. Child received in Baptism and later instructed in the meaning of his or her faith. Involved in ecumenical work.
Statistics*	Membership . . . . 910,297 Congregations . . . . 3,840 *U. S. statistics from *Yearbook of American and Canadian Churches 1998.*	

CHAPTER 7

Church of Christ, Scientist

Mary Baker Eddy founded the Church of Christ, Scientist in 1879 after she was healed of serious injuries as she read a story of healing from Matthew.

Christian Science is a worldwide religion that is based on the Bible, particularly on the teachings and healings of Christ Jesus. A New England woman, Mary Baker Eddy, is the author of the Christian Science textbook, *Science and Health with Key to the Scriptures,* first published in 1875. Eddy saw Christian Science as the law of God, the law of good, that operates universally for the benefit of everyone. *Science and Health* is studied by Christian Scientists, as well as by those of other faiths, in order to make the spiritual meaning of the Bible more understandable.

God is defined not only as the infinite and eternal Being revealed to Moses as "I AM," and as the healing and sustaining power known to Jesus by the intimate name of Father, but also as Mind, Spirit, Truth, Life, Soul, Principle, Love—terms used or implied in the Bible and set forth explicitly in *Science and Health* as synonyms of Deity. God is also understood as Father-Mother, the creative Principle, the source of all that is perfect, indestructible, and immortal. The creation described in the first chapter of Genesis as both wonderfully fresh and flawlessly complete is identified, in Christian Science, as the true creation, inherently good and forever spiritual. All evil and suffering are seen as the result of misunderstanding or ignorance of God.

The True Idea of God

The saving Christ or Son of God is explained as the true idea of God—the divine idea embodied in the life of the historic Jesus and shining through his virgin birth, his healing and teaching ministry, his resurrection following the crucifixion, and his final ascension beyond all material limitations. It is his perfect exemplification of the Christ that makes Jesus' life the way of salvation, the supreme model for all humanity. But, as Christian Scientists understand it, the Christ-power is by no means confined to the person of Jesus, as he himself indicated when he said, "The one who believes in me will also do the works that I do" (John 14:12).

The true idea of God must necessarily include the right understanding of true, individual identity as God's image and likeness, spiritual not material, perfect not fallen. This understanding rescues and reforms us from sin through revealing each individual's true nature—what it means practically, here and now, to be "heirs of God and joint heirs with Christ" as noted in Romans 8:17. As Christian Scientists see it, this understanding is the Holy Spirit, "the Spirit of truth" that Jesus promised would guide "into all the truth" (John 16:13).

How does one gain this Spirit? Through prayer, grace, study, practice—through grasping the spiritual reality beyond material appearances. This enables one, in Paul's words to the Colossians, to take off the "old self" and put on the "new self" whom Christian Science describes as the only real person. This real person, free from sin, disease, and death, has been humanly demonstrated in full perfection only by Christ Jesus, but remains to be demonstrated by all people in proportion to their understanding of Christ's theology and their obedience to Christ's ethics.

As in the New Testament narratives, spiritual healing plays a vital role in Christian Science as a central aspect of Christian salvation. It is not, however, considered miraculous or a matter of blind faith, but the natural result of coming into a more understanding communion with God. Of course, the healing of disease is only a part of the total work to be done. All the sorrow, poverty, crime, injustice, fear, pride, and materialism of human life demand healing. The primary task of the individual, as Christian Science sees it, is to know God, to know oneself as his image, to yield to the Christ-spirit that heals what is unlike God, and increasingly to bring this spiritual understanding to bear on the ills of the world.

Students and Practitioners

A Christian Scientist is apt to speak of himself or herself as a *student* of Christian Science. Like the related word *disciple,* the term implies that Christianity is a study, a discipline, as well as a way of life—a devotion of the heart and soul and mind to understanding God as the very source of one's being.

A Christian Scientist may also be thought of as a *practitioner* of Christian Science. Like the term *minister,* the word suggests that Christianity is a practical ministry, a life of service to humanity—the actual practice of Christian insights in daily life. While the term *Christian Science practitioner* is usually reserved for those who give their full time to the public spiritual healing ministry, every student of Christian Science is expected in a measure to be a practitioner of the faith he or she professes.

Worship and Study

Founded in 1879 by Mary Baker Eddy, the Church of Christ, Scientist is a lay church. Sunday worship services consist of hymns, silent prayer followed by the Lord's Prayer, and a Lesson-Sermon composed of passages from the Bible and *Science and Health* on selected topics. This Bible Lesson is studied during the preceding week by Christian Scientists throughout the world and is read to the congregation on Sunday by two readers who have been elected for this purpose by, and from, the membership of each church. A meeting held on Wednesday evenings includes testimonies of Christian Science healing by members of the congregation, because the sharing of the fruits of spiritual experience is felt to be very important. In Christian Science Sunday schools young people learn the relevance of the Bible to their daily lives. Other resources and activities provided by churches of Christ, Scientist, for their communities include Reading Rooms and public lectures on Christian Science.

The Church of Christ, Scientist is involved in a variety of ecumenical discussions at both local and national levels worldwide.

For Discussion	
	□ What do you think of Christian Science teachings on healing, in light of Jesus' healing miracles and of today's medical science? □ How do you react to the statement "All evil and suffering are seen as the result of misunderstanding or ignorance of God"? □ Lutheran theology teaches that the old, sinful self is very real; Christian Science would disagree. Where would you stand on that question, and why?

For Further Study

The following books are available at Christian Science Reading Rooms and public libraries:

□ *Science and Health with Key to the Scriptures* by Mary Baker Eddy (Boston: The Christian Science Board of Directors, 1994)

□ *Healing Spiritually: Renewing Your Life Through the Power of God's Law* (Boston: The Christian Science Publishing Society, 1996)

□ *Mary Baker Eddy: Christian Healer* by Yvonne Cache von Fettweis and Robert Townsend Warneck (Boston: The Christian Science Publishing Society, 1998)

□ Christian Scientist Web sites: www.tfcc.com and www.marybakereddy.org

Table of Comparison	*Christian Scientists*	*Lutherans*
Teachings	1. Accept the Bible and *Science and Health with Key to the Scriptures* by Mary Baker Eddy as their textbooks and pastor.	1. Accept the Bible as the written witness to God's revelation of saving action through Jesus Christ.
	2. Understand the three aspects of the trinity as God, the Father-Mother; His Son, one Christ; and the Holy Ghost or divine Comforter.	2. Maintain classic doctrine of triune God: Father, Son, and Holy Spirit.
	3. Believe sin, sickness, and death result from ignorance or misunderstanding of God, and that these are overcome through a right understanding of God.	3. Believe in the reality of sin, with sickness and death present because of evil.
	4. Believe God's creation is wholly spiritual and good.	4. Believe in the reality of God's creation; affirm humankind's creative responsibility within creation.
Type of Worship	A Sunday service consisting of hymns, prayers, and a Lesson-Sermon comprised of selections from the Bible and *Science and Health* read by two lay Readers. A Wednesday evening meeting that includes testimonies of Christian Science healing.	Liturgical patterns of worship used, led by an ordained minister with preaching of the Word and celebration of sacraments involving elements of water, bread, and wine.
Government	Organized under the *Church Manual* by Mary Baker Eddy, comprised of The First Church of Christ, Scientist, in Boston (The Mother Church), together with local, democratically-governed branch churches of Christ, Scientist, worldwide.	Interdependent congregational, regional, national, and global expressions of the church characterized by democratic decision making, strong ecumenical relationships, elected leadership, and an ordained ministry.
Characteristics	Emphasis on spiritual understanding of God, Christian virtues, and healing of physical, moral, and societal ills through spiritual means, as exemplified by Christ Jesus.	Emphasis on salvation by grace through faith apart from works of the law. Physical healing seen as God working through natural means and medical care.
Statistics	In accordance with the *Manual,* no church membership figures are reported for publication. As of 1999, there are about 2,200 Christian Science branch churches in 74 countries.	

CHAPTER 8

Church of God

Teachings from the New Testament provide the standard of faith and life for individuals in the Church of God.

More than a million Americans are associated with a Church of God group of some kind. Actually, most of these groups (some 200 independent bodies) have little in common with each other except for their common use of a New Testament name for the church. Almost all, however, are relatively young bodies with recent American origins, frequently with a common emphasis on the work of the Holy Spirit to empower and guide people.

This movement has a concern for Christian unity, holy living, and the use of the New Testament as the standard of faith and life. It grew out of a belief that the church was too restricted and burdened by organization and should be more directly under the "rule of God."

The church is seen as the body of Christ on earth. Baptism of believers by immersion, communion, and foot washing are understood to be simply reminders or object lessons about how God works with God's people. The Church of God has no written creed, but has sought to be guided by consensus as to the clear teachings of the Bible. This has left much to individual interpretation and has produced personalized faith. Worship practices vary a great deal from congregation to congregation and even from service to service. There is no established liturgy, but worship is carried out with varying degrees of formality.

A unique characteristic of this movement is its attitude toward formal church membership. Out of a feeling that only Christ may accept people into the spiritual body of the church, Church of God congregations maintain no formal membership rolls. It is felt that only when people commit themselves to Christ do they become a part of the church. Only in God's judgment and not in that of leaders of a congregation is someone considered to be a member.

For Discussion

□ In general, Churches of God have stressed the work of the Holy Spirit, and Lutherans have stressed the work of Jesus Christ. How do you think these different emphases may have shaped the denominations?
□ What are the benefits and drawbacks of the Church of God approach to membership?

For Further Study
□ *The Church of God: A Social History* by Mickey Crews (Knoxville: University of Tennessee Press, 1990)
□ Church of God in Christ web site: www.cogic.com

Table of Comparison	*Church of God*	*Lutherans*
Teachings	1. The Bible is God's Word.	1. The Bible is the written witness to God's revelation of saving purpose through Jesus Christ.
	2. Humankind is justified by faith in Christ's work.	2. Same.
	3. Believe in God as personal; Christ as God's Son, fully human, fully divine; and the Holy Spirit doing God's work on earth among humankind. Give special emphasis to the work of the Spirit as strengthener and guide.	3. Same, but emphasis placed upon Christ. Spirit given in baptism, not in a special event as affirmed by pentecostal Churches of God.
	4. People can grow in commitment to live the Christian life and can find their motivations made more like the purpose of God through the Spirit in sanctification.	4. Christian life is growth in grace, but perfection never completed in this life.
	5. Three ordinances: baptism of believers by immersion, communion, and foot washing.	5. Two sacraments: Baptism of infants or adults for the forgiveness of sin; and the Lord's Supper to celebrate the real presence of Christ.
Type of Worship	No set form but generally not liturgical. Degree of pattern varies widely.	Liturgical worship patterns following the tradition of the Western church.
Government	Mixture of congregational and presbyterian. Local churches call their own ministers. Pastors ordained by state or area assemblies.	Interdependent congregational, regional, national, and global expressions of the church characterized by democratic decision making, strong ecumenical relationships, elected leadership, and an ordained ministry.
Statistics	Membership* (based on 10 Churches of God) .... 6,721,748 Churches .... 27,699 *More than 200 bodies bear the name *Church of God*. The Church of God in Christ (headquarters in Memphis, Tenn.) is the largest, with an inclusive membership of around 5.5 million. (U. S. statistics from *Yearbook of American and Canadian Churches 1998*.)	

CHAPTER 9

Church of the Brethren

The love feast *or communion service (an ordinance in Church of the Brethren) includes a foot washing ceremony symbolizing servanthood.*

The Church of the Brethren is one of the older denominations in the *Believers Church* or *Free Church* tradition. Originating in 1708 as a separatist movement among German Pietists, Brethren were strongly influenced by Anabaptism (see the chapter on the Mennonite Church). By 1735 the Brethren had migrated from Germany to colonial America, where they were often called "Dunkers" because of their distinctive practice of threefold immersion baptism of adult believers. Their Germanic culture, strict social, ethic, and pacifist convictions kept them isolated from mainstream American life until the latter half of the nineteenth century. By that time they had expanded to the West Coast, with no congregations, however, in New England and few in the Deep South.

Brethren accept the Bible as the trustworthy Word of God to which they teach obedience. Most Brethren take the New Testament as a higher and more complete revelation than the Old Testament, while still affirming the unity of the scriptures. Brethren accept the basic tenets of Protestant Christianity but are noncreedal in a strict sense. They do on occasion use the traditional creeds as "affirmations of faith."

Church practices are usually referred to as *ordinances* (commandments of the Lord) rather than sacraments. They include baptism by immersion, a love feast or communion (with foot washing after John 13:3-17, a fellowship meal, and the eucharist), and anointing for spiritual and bodily health.

Brethren have been active in higher education, publishing, and world missions. Former mission congregations in India, China, Nigeria, and Ecuador have become independent bodies related to national churches. Brethren have been particularly known for a worldwide program of social welfare, relief and reconstruction, and peace activities. Although Brethren teach Christian pacifism, members who enter the military service remain in good standing. The Church of the Brethren is a member of the National and World Councils of Churches.

For Discussion

□ How do you think the old nickname "Dunkers" reflects common attitudes toward faith traditions we don't understand?

□ Would you argue that it is wise or unwise for Christians to keep somewhat separate from aspects of society? Why?

For Further Study

□ *Meet the Brethren* ed. Donald F. Durnbaugh (Elgin, Ill.: Brethren Press, 1984)

□ *Against the Wind: Eberhard Arnold and the Bruderhof* by Markus Baum and Jim Wallis (Plough Publishing House, 1998)

□ Brethren web site: www.brethren.org

Table of Comparison	*Brethren*	*Lutherans*
Teachings	1. Believe the Bible is the trustworthy Word of God. 2. Believe in the triune nature of God. 3. Believe in the full divinity and full humanity of Christ. 4. Are noncreedal but accept the creeds as nonbinding "affirmations of faith." 5. Practice the ordinances of believer's baptism; love feast including foot washing, meal, and communion; and anointing. 6. Teach Christian pacifism.	1. Accept the Bible as the written witness to God's revelation of saving action through Jesus Christ. 2. Same. 3. Same. 4. Subscribe to the ecumenical creeds: Apostles', Nicene, and Athanasian. 5. Celebrate two sacraments: Baptism, including infants, and Holy Communion. 6. Pacifism not taught as a basic Christian position.
Type of Worship	A mixture of "low church" and more liturgical forms.	Liturgical, following the primary patterns of the Western church.
Government	Combination of congregational and presbyterian polity.	Interdependent congregational, regional, national, and global expressions of the church characterized by democratic decision making, strong ecumenical relationships, elected leadership, and an ordained ministry.
Characteristics	Major emphasis on Christian life and ethics.	Emphasis on doctrine with life and ethics to be shaped by faith.
Statistics*	Membership . . . . 141,811 Congregations . . . . 1,106 *U. S. statistics from *Yearbook of American and Canadian Churches 1998.*	

CHAPTER 10

Church of the Nazarene

Trained evangelists who go door-to-door help the Church of the Nazarene grow.

The Church of the Nazarene started on October 8, 1908, when three holiness groups from the East, the West, and the South united. This culminated a movement that began in the nineteenth century to conserve and spread the doctrine of holiness.

Strongly biblical in emphasis, the Church of the Nazarene is Arminian-Wesleyan in theology. Therefore, the doctrine of entire sanctification, which teaches cleansing from inborn sin now, is particularly significant to the denomination.

Everyone is believed to be born with a nature adverse to God and inclined toward evil. The Holy Spirit makes people aware of their sin and provides *prevenient* grace (grace in anticipation of repentance) that enables them to turn from their sin in repentance and have faith in Christ. This conversion experience is the beginning of the Christian life in the believer. It is followed by spiritual growth. At some point in the Christian pilgrimage every believer realizes that even though God has forgiven his or her sins there remains an inner inclination toward evil. The Holy Spirit draws the Christian to commit his or her life completely to God. When Christians respond in faith to this call to consecration, they are entirely sanctified. This means they are cleansed from the inclination toward evil and are "perfected in love" for God.

The whole Christian church is said to include all spiritually regenerate persons. "The Church of the Nazarene is composed of those persons who have voluntarily associated themselves together according to the doctrine and polity of said church...." Members are admitted on the basis of their confession of faith and their agreement to submit to the church's government.

Two ordinances are observed: baptism by sprinkling, pouring, or most often immersion, and the Lord's supper. Baptism is administered to believers as a sign of their faith in Christ and their intent to follow Christ. Young children may be baptized upon the request of parents who give assurance for them of necessary Christian training.

The Lord's supper is considered a memorial of Christ's sacrificial death. As the communion feast, it is only for those who have faith in Christ and are living the Christian life. Communicants receive both the unleavened bread and the nonfermented wine.

Traditionally, worship in the church has been characterized by freedom and personal involvement. Both music and preaching play important roles in worship services.

For Discussion

□ What do you think of the idea that Christians can become completely sanctified—perfected in love—in this life?

□ The Nazarene practice of baptism seems to be a mix of infant baptism and believer's baptism. Compare the theology behind this with that of your church's baptismal practice.

For Further Study

□ Nazarene Web site: www.nazarene.org

Table of Comparison	*Nazarene*	*Lutherans*
Teachings	1. Original sin may be cleansed in the work of entire sanctification. This work of grace is after regeneration and is possible in this life.	1. Christian life is growth in forgiveness, but perfection never completed in this life.
	2. All spiritually regenerate persons are members of the church.	2. The church exists where God's Word is preached and the sacraments are rightly administered.
	3. Baptism and the Lord's supper are considered signs of faith.	3. Sacraments of Baptism and Lord's Supper are means of grace. Real presence of Christ affirmed in Communion.
	4. The Bible is seen as the divinely inspired Word of God.	4. The Bible is the written witness to God's revelation of saving action through Jesus Christ.
	5. Believe in the triune nature of God as well as the full divinity and humanity of Christ.	5. Same.
	6. Salvation is possible only through personal faith in the atonement for sin made by Jesus Christ.	6. Salvation by grace through faith apart from works of the law is taught.
Type of Worship	Characterized by freedom and personal involvement. Emphasis on preaching with strong evangelistic stress.	Liturgical following the Western pattern with both the preaching of the gospel and the celebration of the sacraments considered important.
Government	Representative in form, local congregation selects pastor and manages own affairs. Governing boards elected by supervising group.	Interdependent congregational, regional, national, and global expressions of the church characterized by democratic decision making, strong ecumenical relationships, elected leadership, and an ordained ministry.
Characteristics	Major emphasis on personal holiness rather than upon group social action. Not involved in ecumenical movement, but cooperates with other groups of similar doctrine and practice.	Works cooperatively for the ministry of the church. Socially aware, seeking greater understanding and offering the strength of its heritage.
Statistics*	Membership . . . . 608,008 Congregations . . . . 5,135 *U. S. statistics from *Yearbook of American and Canadian Churches 1998.*	

CHAPTER 11

Eastern Orthodox Church

In the Eastern church, the Sacrament of Holy Communion is administered by a spoon from a chalice where the leavened bread and wine have been mixed together.

Eastern Orthodoxy made an atypical entrance into North America. Although most immigrants came first to the East Coast and gradually moved westward by covered wagon, Eastern Orthodoxy traveled in the opposite direction. Russian Orthodox missionaries established a mission in 1794 on Kodiak Island off the coast of Alaska. When the United States purchased that territory from Russia, these Orthodox missionaries spread their work from Alaska as far south as San Francisco. Later their work moved to Minneapolis where they started a seminary, and from there Orthodoxy went eastward to Pennsylvania, New York, and other states.

Three Basic Groups

Worldwide, the Eastern church constitutes the third largest body of Christians, with approximately 170 million Orthodox Christians. There are three main groups of Eastern Christians: (1) the *Eastern Orthodox,* such as the Greek and Russian churches; (2) the *Oriental Orthodox,* such as the Copts and the Armenians who separated from the Byzantine Orthodox in the fifth century for ethnic and theological reasons; and (3) the *Greek Catholic* or Uniate churches, which are in union with Rome, such as the Melchites and Maronites. This chapter considers only the first group, the Eastern Orthodox Church.

From the Apostles

The Eastern Orthodox Church dates its existence from the time of the apostles. It was the apostle Paul, for example, who established the Christian church in Greece through his early missionary journeys. The apostle Peter founded the church in Antioch. Other apostles established the church in Jerusalem, Alexandria, and Cyprus. The Eastern Orthodox Church has existed in these places since apostolic times. From these cities and countries, missionaries brought the gospel of Christ to many other countries including Russia and the Ukraine.

In this way, the family of churches known as Eastern Orthodox was born: the Syrian, Greek, Ukrainian, Russian, Bulgarian, Serbian, Romanian, Albanian, and so forth. Although these churches govern themselves independently and use their own native language in the liturgy, they share the same worship service, the same sacraments, and the same beliefs. The Patriarch of Constantinople is recognized by all Eastern Orthodox Churches as the spiritual head of the church in *honor* only. He has no authority comparable to that of the pope. The bishops of all the orthodox churches in the world meet together when necessary to discuss common problems. Their meeting is called an ecumenical council.

English is replacing the many foreign languages used in the liturgy for the some four million Orthodox Christians in the United States. Although the various Orthodox churches in America still govern themselves independently, there is co-operation on matters of religious education, campus ministry, and chaplaincy work.

Orthodox Means...

The word *orthodox,* meaning "true belief," was given to the Eastern church because of its efforts in the early days of Christianity to preserve the true faith of Christ. When the Christian faith was challenged by false teachers in the early centuries, it was the Eastern church that took the initiative to call together the first seven ecumenical councils that defined and explained some of the basic beliefs of Christianity. All of these councils were called together by the East and met in the East. Some of the major decrees of these councils accepted by Orthodox Christians today are: the divinity of Christ, the two natures of Christ—divine and human—united in one person, and the Nicene Creed, which is the official creed of the Eastern Orthodox Church.

Worship Amid Joy

The Eastern Orthodox Church has always placed great emphasis on worship; its services are longer in duration than the worship services of most Christian churches in the West. Its main worship service—the liturgy—has captured that element of sheer joy in the resurrection of the Lord Jesus that is found in the writings of the early church. It has been said that one of the main characteristics of the Eastern church is its power to perceive the celestial beauty of the spiritual world and to express it in worship.

The importance of the liturgy in Eastern Orthodoxy is that it is the means by which a person communes with the Lord Jesus. In the first part of the liturgy, the Eastern Christian communes with Christ as the Word of God. This section consists essentially on readings from the Holy Scriptures followed by their explanation in the sermon, an important element of the liturgy. Through the scripture lessons and the sermon, Christ himself speaks to the people. A personal encounter with the living Christ occurs.

In the second part of the liturgy, the worshiper communes with Christ as the Bread of Life. He or she receives the body and blood of Jesus through the Sacrament of Communion. Both communions—the encounter with Christ as the Word and Christ as the Bread of Life—are ways of partaking of Christ. Both are achieved through the liturgy as it is celebrated every Sunday and on major feast days.

The central event of the liturgy is the descent, the appearance, the divine presence of the resurrected Christ. A person is frequently reminded of this presence. For example, at one point in the liturgy the priest says, "Christ is with us." And the assistant priest responds, after exchanging the kiss of peace, with "He is with us and will ever be."

Orthodox worship services appeal to the whole person through the five senses: *sight,* through the visual beauty of the icons (religious paintings) and vestments; *smell,* through the use of incense; *sound,* through the music of the Orthodox liturgy; *taste,* through the Sacrament of Holy Communion and drinking of holy water; *touch,* by crossing oneself, kissing the icon, and lighting candles on entering an Orthodox church.

Seven Mysteries

The word for *sacrament* in Greek is *mysterion,* meaning "mystery." Seven "mysteries" or sacraments are practiced in the Orthodox church together with sacramentals, or lesser sacraments. Two examples of sacramentals are the blessing of holy water, and the tonsure (shaved heads) of monks. The word *mystery* expresses a fundamental characteristic of the Orthodox church: its emphasis on the mystery of God. No attempt is made to define what is indefinable in God.

The Orthodox church is willing to accept the mystery of what happens to the bread and wine in Holy Communion without trying to define how it happens. The word *transubstantiation* is used, but it is one of many terms utilized to describe the change. They insist, however, as Metropolitan Philaret of Moscow wrote, that "the bread truly, really, and substantially becomes the very true body of our Lord, and the wine the very true blood of our Lord."

Applied to the sacraments, the word *mystery* denotes the mysterious way God brings grace and love to us through these channels. The seven sacraments are

□ *Communion.* In the Eastern church, the Sacrament of Holy Communion is administered by a spoon from a chalice where the leavened bread and wine have been mixed together.

□ *Baptism.* The Sacrament of Baptism is administered in infancy by the total immersion of the naked infant in the baptismal font. This is done in the name of the Holy Trinity. Orthodox Christians usually wear a small cross as a reminder of their baptism.

□ *Confirmation.* The Sacrament of Confirmation is administered immediately following Baptism. The newly baptized and confirmed infant becomes a full member of the church and begins to receive Holy Communion from the time of Baptism. The same Holy Spirit who descended upon the apostles at Pentecost descends upon the newly baptized in confirmation, granting them a share in the royal priesthood of Christ.

□ *Confession.* The Sacrament of Confession takes the form of a private conference between the priest and the penitent. The penitent kneels before an icon of the Savior. The priest, standing behind or beside the penitent, also faces the icon. This outward form emphasizes that it is not the priest but God who is the judge. After making one's confession to Christ, the priest pronounces Christ's forgiveness upon the penitent.

□ *Holy Unction.* The Sacrament of Holy Unction is conferred on any person who is sick. This sacrament consists of prayer and the anointing of the sick with consecrated oil.

□ *Holy Orders.* The Sacrament of Holy Orders is performed by the bishop. The three Major Orders in the Orthodox church are bishop, priest, and deacon. Priests and deacons may be either married or unmarried. If they are to be married, they must choose the state of marriage before ordination. Marriage is not permitted after ordination; however, bishops are elected only from the unmarried clergy.

□ *Matrimony.* The Sacrament of Holy Matrimony is a very colorful sacrament in which the bride and groom receive Christ's blessing. Like the five wise maidens in the Bible, the couple hold candles throughout the ceremony to express their eagerness to receive the Bridegroom, Christ, as he comes to bless them through this sacrament. They drink wine from the same cup, signifying that they will share everything in life. They also are crowned with a crown of leaves or one of silver and gold to emphasize the special grace of the Holy Spirit who "crowns" them with glory and honor as king and queen of their small kingdom, their home.

Orthodox Customs

The *Antidoron,* a little piece of bread, is received by worshipers from the priest at the conclusion of each liturgy. This bread is blessed but not consecrated, although taken from the same loaf as the bread used in the consecration. In many Orthodox parishes, non-Orthodox people present at the liturgy are encouraged to receive the Antidoron as an expression of Christian fellowship and love.

Christmas is observed on January 7 by some Orthodox churches, notably the Russian, Ukrainian, Serbian, and Bulgarian, since they still follow the old Julian calendar. The Greek, Syrian, and Romanian churches, having adopted the Gregorian calendar, celebrate Christmas on December 25.

The date of Easter also does not often coincide with that of the West. Usually it occurs a week or more later. This practice stems from the Eastern Orthodox interpretation of Scripture in which the resurrection of Jesus is believed to have occurred *following* the Jewish Passover.

Icons

The Eastern church makes extensive use of icons—religious paintings of Christ and the saints. During the early history of the church, the iconoclasts (icon breakers) set out to destroy all icons. They felt that it was idolatrous to paint a picture of God who is eternal and invisible. The Orthodox Christians, on the other hand, insisted that God could be painted because he had become a person in Jesus. Because of this, it was lawful to make a picture of him.

Icons have been called prayers, hymns, and sermons in form and color. They are the visual gospel. In an Orthodox church the faithful may see unfolded before them in paintings on the walls and ceiling almost all the mysteries of the Christian religion. Orthodox Christians use icons in their homes as a reminder of God's presence and for family prayer.

Bible and Tradition

A distinctive feature of the Orthodox church is its loyalty to tradition. The Eastern church recognizes two sources of faith: Scripture and Sacred Tradition. Sacred Tradition does not mean the tradition of human beings or a slavish attachment to the past, but a living connection with the entire past experience of the church. It includes all that the Holy Spirit has taught and continues to teach through the church. More specifically, Sacred Tradition means the books of the Bible, the Nicene Creed, the decrees of the Ecumenical Councils, and the writings of the Church Fathers.

The Orthodox church is a scriptural church. It considers the Bible as the supreme expression of God's revelation to humankind. The Bible, therefore, occupies a unique preeminence (superiority) within Sacred Tradition. So does the Nicene Creed. These are absolute and cannot be canceled or revised. Other parts of Sacred Tradition such as the Canons, the service books, and the icons do not have the same authority and can be changed.

Source of Authority	The highest authority of the Eastern church is the Ecumenical Council, involving the whole church. When the bishops define a matter of faith in an Ecumenical Council, their decision must be accepted by the lay people of the church as a whole. Only then can it be considered infallible or inspired of the Holy Spirit, who resides in the whole church, consisting of clergy and laity, to guide it to all truth. This makes every person within the church responsible for Christian truth.
Communion of Saints	The idea of the communion of saints, the saints on earth communing with the saints in heaven, is greatly emphasized in the Eastern church. This communion is expressed very effectively in the way the icons are placed on the walls of the Orthodox church. Below the figure of Christ on the top of the dome are painted on the walls and apse (altar area), the members of the *church triumphant* in heaven—the Virgin Mary, the prophets, the angels, and the apostles. Finally, on the floor level of the church are the living saints, the members of the *church militant on earth*. Thus, around the figure of Christ in the dome is gathered the entire church, both that in heaven and that on earth. Eastern Christians are constantly reminded that they are members of a great body. As such they do not feel alone when they pray as members of the body of Christ—the church triumphant is praying with them.
Response in Service	Eastern Orthodoxy believes that the thankful Christian is one who responds to God for what God has done in Christ. This response is *diakonia*—service to one's neighbor. What is faith without deeds? As a result of this awareness, the Orthodox church teaches that personal salvation expresses itself in social concern, inviting the Christian to be a servant to all people for Christ's sake.
For Discussion	□ Even though its liturgy is elaborate and rarely embraces change, the Eastern Orthodox church has grown rapidly in recent years. Why do you think this might be so? □ What characteristics about traditional icons catch your eye? Do you think they could aid in your own worship? □ What is similar between your church and Eastern Orthodoxy? What is different? ***For Further Study*** □ *The Orthodox Way* by Kallistos Ware (St. Vladimir's Seminary Press, 1995) □ *Introducing the Orthodox Church* by Anthony M. Coniaris (Minneapolis: Light and Life Publishing, 1982) □ Eastern Orthodox Church Web site: www.oca.org

Table of Comparison	*Eastern Orthodox*	*Lutherans*
Teachings	1. Accept the original Nicene Creed, which did not include the filioque phrase.* Orthodox Christians believe that the Holy Spirit proceeds only from the Father and is sent through the Son. 2. Accept Bible and seven general councils as authority. Tradition valid for church. 3. Celebrate seven sacraments. 4. Believe in transubstantiation, that is, the bread and wine in Communion are changed into the body and blood of Christ. 5. Maintain apostolic succession in that priests must be ordained in an unbroken line back to the apostles.	1. Same, with addition of Western filioque phrase. The Western church believes that the Holy Spirit proceeds from the Father and the Son. 2. Accept the Bible as authority, expressed in creeds and confessions. 3. Celebrate two sacraments: Baptism and Holy Communion. 4. Believe in consubstantiation, that is, the communicant receives the body and blood of Christ with the bread and wine. 5. Apostolic succession is understood as continuity with the apostles' teaching.
Type of Worship	Highly liturgical with Eastern Rite. Usually in the language of the people but not always so.	Liturgical but follows the tradition and services of the Western church. Language of people used.
Government	An episcopal form of government with bishops, priests, and deacons. Patriarchs and archbishops occupy the more important bishoprics, but are not more important in theory.	Interdependent congregational, regional, national, and global expressions of the church characterized by democratic decision making, strong ecumenical relationships, elected leadership, and an ordained ministry.
Characteristics	Great emphasis on the drama of the liturgy, on the family, and the nation. Church often closely related to government in parts of the world.	Liturgy seen as a means of worship and a resource for life. Church usually separate from government today, except in parts of Europe.
Statistics[†]	Membership .... 5,013,821 Congregations 1,678	

* *Filioque* is Latin for "and the Son." Thus, the original, and still the Orthodox version, states in the third article, "...who proceeds from the Father. With the Father and the Son...."

† U. S. statistics from *Yearbook of American and Canadian Churches 1998*. Note that one major branch, the Russian Orthodox Church Outside of Russia, did not report any membership numbers.

CHAPTER 12

Episcopal Church

Henry VIII won permission from Parliament to become the head of the Church in England, thus making it independent of papal control.

It is sometimes hard for non-Episcopalians to figure out just what the Episcopal Church is all about. Sometimes Episcopalians seem to be more like Catholics; sometimes they seem not much different from Protestants. Occasionally, they refer to themselves as *high church* or *low church*. Even their church buildings reveal differences: one building will be elaborately furnished, while another will look as simple as a New England meeting house. Some Episcopal clergy wear colorful vestments; others do not. Why all the variations?

Political in Origin

The Episcopal Church looks the way it does—and believes what it believes, for that matter—because of its history. It came into being as a separate denomination not so much for theological reasons, but more for political and jurisdictional ones. A look at the origins of its parent, the Church of England, is necessary if we are to understand the Episcopal Church.

Though the Church in England developed independently, by the time of the Reformation it had long been aligned with Rome. It might have remained so, except for some very special religious and political events in the sixteenth century. The political events can be summed up in two words: *money* and *monarchy*.

Henry VII took over the throne of England in 1485 after a long and bitter civil war, but he did not have a sound legal right to do so. Fearful of another civil war, his son, King Henry VIII, decided that he needed a male heir to make certain his family continued in power. In other words, he wanted a son. But Henry and his wife had only a daughter. So it was that Henry VIII asked the pope in Rome for an *annulment* (that is, a setting aside) of his marriage to Catherine of Aragon. Popes had in the past been willing to grant annulments of royal marriages, particularly when the question of heirs to the throne came up. But, unfortunately, the pope to whom Henry appealed was, at that moment, the political prisoner of the King of Spain, who happened to be Catherine's nephew. The pope, quite understandably, did not wish to offend his captor and refused Henry's request.

Henry thereupon adopted a different strategy. He won permission from Parliament to become the head of the Church in England, thus making it independent of papal control. Once he had done so, the English Church granted him the annulment he sought. The king's treasury also benefited from the independence of the church. The very large amounts of money that had formerly gone to the pope now went to Henry. In 1533 the king remarried, and another daughter (the future Elizabeth I) was born to him. His second wife—the famous Anne Boleyn—was executed a few years later for treason, and Henry married a third time. Of this marriage, finally, a son was born.

Monarchs and the Church

When Henry VIII died, his 10-year-old son, Edward VI, succeeded him. Under Edward, the Church of England came strongly under the influence of German and Swiss Reformers. Edward was only a boy, and his advisers, chief among them Archbishop of Canterbury Thomas Cranmer, were themselves sympathetic to Lutheran and Calvinist ideas. Under Henry's direction the Bible had been translated into English and parts of the church's services were spoken in English. But under Edward the use of Latin was abolished, and a *Book of Common Prayer* was issued and ordered to be used throughout England. In many parts of that Prayer Book, one can see evidence of reformed theology. While Henry was king, there were very few theological changes in the beliefs of the Church of England, but during Edward's reign, the influence of the Reformers was growing. If Edward had reigned for a long time, the English church might have developed into a Reformed church.

However, Edward VI lived only six years after coming to the throne. When he died, Henry's older daughter, Mary I, the child of Catherine of Aragon, succeeded him. She was a devout Roman Catholic, and during her reign the Church of England was returned to papal control. Eager to demonstrate her loyalty to the pope, Mary executed Cranmer, the author of the *Book of Common Prayer,* and burned at the stake two other reforming bishops, Hugh Latimer and Nicholas Ridley. When she died, unhappy and unloved by her subjects, the throne went to Henry's second daughter, Elizabeth I.

Probably because the reigns of her half-brother and half-sister had been marked by a great deal of religious intolerance, Elizabeth wanted the English church to make room both for Protestants and Catholics, with neither side dominating. Under the resulting so-called Elizabethan Settlement, the church retained much of its Roman Catholic heritage. Church government, for instance, remained like that of the old days, with bishops, priests, and deacons. A Roman Catholic understanding of the sacraments was retained, but certain concessions were made to the reformers. Fundamental Christian doctrines, such as that of the incarnation, were carefully retained. On the other hand, the Bible and the services were required to be read in English, not Latin. Clergy were allowed to marry.

The Elizabethan Settlement did not ease all of the hard feelings. Indeed, even today there are individuals and groups within the Episcopal Church who, like the reformers and the Roman Catholics of Elizabeth's time, would like to see more of one tradition or the other. The church, however, officially retains both Roman Catholic and Protestant elements, as well as vestiges of its original Celtic spirit.

Episcopal Church in America

As English colonists came to America, they brought their church with them, although, of course, the Pilgrims who settled Massachusetts Bay Colony were Protestant refugees from the religious conflict in England. After the American

Revolution, the American branch of the Anglican church broke its formal ties with the English church and became an independent, national church. But like other, similar offshoots of the English church (in Canada, Australia, and New Zealand, for instance), the Episcopal Church remains part of what is called the Anglican Communion—that is, the group of national churches sharing the same historical bond and the same understanding of Christianity.

No Theological Label

Given its background, it is no wonder that the Episcopal Church cannot be described by any one particular theological label. These variations of interpretation have come to be considered as quite normal. But its theology is not much different from that of other Christian bodies.

The doctrine of the Trinity—God as Father, Son, and Holy Spirit—is central, and Episcopalians use both the Nicene and the Apostles' Creeds as affirmations of this doctrine. Human beings, according to Anglican belief, were—and are—created free. But they have rebelled against their creator. Their rebellion has left them isolated and fearful, unable to get back to God by their own efforts. The incarnation united the human race with God, and the crucifixion and resurrection overcame the power of humanity's rebellious nature. The church continues to do the work of God on earth by continuing the work of Christ.

Scripture and Tradition

The Episcopal Church looks both to Holy Scripture and to tradition as the means by which we can understand how God's work of salvation is accomplished. Holy Scripture, it is agreed, contains everything necessary for Christian belief, but tradition enriches and interprets scripture.

The Episcopalian's attitude toward the sacraments and sacramental acts provides an example of the way in which scripture and tradition work within the church. Sacraments are the special means by which God unites with humans and helps them live Christian lives in a difficult world. Holy Baptism, for instance, gives people a new start. In this sacrament, God breaks the hold of sin on human life and makes the individual person a part of the church. Holy Communion renews the relationship with God and the church that was given in Baptism. Episcopalians believe in the presence of Christ in the bread and wine of the Eucharist, but the way in which Christ is present is not considered to be of great importance.

Only these two sacraments, Baptism and the Eucharist, were ordained by Christ as shown in the scriptures, so the Episcopal Church regards only these two as necessary for salvation. However, Christian tradition, as far back as the apostles' time, has singled out other special acts and events as sacramental. As understood by the Episcopal Church, these sacramental helps are

□ *Confirmation,* in which the vows of Baptism are renewed in a sort of ordination in the life of a mature Christian;

□ *Reconciliation of a Penitent,* or confession of sins in the presence of a priest, who assures the pardon and grace of absolution;

□ *Ordination,* which confers authority and the grace of the Holy Spirit to those who are to serve God and the church in the ordained ministry;

□ *Holy Matrimony,* for those who are being married; and

□ *Unction of the sick,* which provides God's help for the sick as well as for the dying.

These five sacramental *helps* or *graces* are like the sacraments described in the Bible because they make use of visible signs and actions as channels for God's love and power; however, these sacramental helps were not commanded by Christ as necessary for the Christian life. They are part of a tradition that forms a portion of the church's life. Many Episcopalians make use of these sacramental helps, but no one is required to do so.

Worship: Book of Common Prayer

Worship in the Episcopal Church is based on the *Book of Common Prayer,* although different parishes follow different traditions in their use of the options available in the Prayer Book. The central act of worship is the Holy Eucharist, or Holy Communion. In most cases, Episcopalian services are liturgical in nature. That is, there is more or less a fixed form that always includes congregational participation. From place to place, the fixed form may be enriched with extra prayers, ceremonies, and music; alternatively, the form may be kept quite simple, with nothing added to the Prayer Book rite. The more elaborate services are sometimes called "high church"; the simpler ones, "low church." To an extent, these variations reflect the denomination's conflicted history.

While a good deal of freedom is allowed in local parishes concerning worship as well as a diversity of theological views among individual Episcopalians, the structure of the Episcopal Church helps to keep all varieties of belief and worship under one roof.

Three Orders of Clergy

Following the Roman Catholic tradition, the Episcopal Church has three orders of clergy. It has bishops, whose connection with the original apostles is maintained in the historical episcopate. Bishops must be elected by a majority vote of both the clergy and the laity of a diocese. That election must then be approved by a majority of bishops and dioceses in the church before the election is validated. Bishops ordain clergy and administer confirmation. Priests, or presbyters, are men and women who work mostly as pastors of parishes. Their primary job is to administer the sacraments, to preach, and to teach. The third order is the diaconate. Deacons assist priests. Their ordination is sometimes seen as something like a doctor's internship; after a certain length of time, many deacons are ordained as priests. Others remain in what is known as the perpetual diaconate, a ministry devoted to acts of service, particularly to the poor, the sick, and the lonely. Lay readers are people licensed to conduct certain services and to help with the administration of Holy Communion.

Ecumenical Participation

In recent years the ecumenical movement has been one of the major concerns of Episcopalians. It has been active in organizations such as the National Council of Churches and the Consultation on Church Union. The General Convention has endorsed Episcopal Church efforts toward ecumenism, though no actual merger with other denominations is anticipated.

An example of the direction in which such efforts are leading is the interim sharing of the Eucharist among the Episcopal Church and the Evangelical Lutheran Church in America. This agreement was sanctioned by the General Convention in 1982. The two churches are, as of this writing, working toward full communion, that is, the joint recognition of the members and clergy of each other's denomination. Importantly, given its history, Episcopalians are concerned that ecumenical efforts also include Roman Catholics. The Anglican-Roman

Catholic International Consultation (ARCIC) has led to the preparation of papers that describe points of agreement, as well as areas for concern and future study. These actions indicate the desire on the part of all Anglicans, including Episcopalians, to close the gaps between the churches.

Facing World Problems

For many years the church has maintained social agencies, hospitals, and schools in an effort to ease human needs. Episcopal friars, monks, and nuns, for instance, have done much selfless work in slum parishes and in education for the poor. The General Convention has allocated millions of dollars for work in urban ghetto situations, in Latin America, and Africa. Parishes in the cities have received much attention, both on the national and the diocesan level. The Presiding Bishop's Fund for World Relief works both alone and ecumenically in dealing with both domestic and foreign crises of hunger, refugee resettlement, and development.

Because of its English roots, the Episcopal Church remained for many years a predominantly white Anglo-Saxon church. Over the last century, however, a concerted effort has been made to reach out to the African American, Asian, American Indian, and Hispanic communities. A significant number of parishes now bring the Anglican tradition and worship to a new constituency. Indeed, today the majority of Anglicans in the world are people of color.

For Discussion

□ How does the Episcopal Church's development as a separate denomination compare with that of your church body?
□ What are some similarities and differences between Episcopal teachings and those of your church? Are the differences important?
□ Do you think you would feel comfortable worshiping in an Episcopal church? Why or why not?

For Further Study

□ *Looking at the Episcopal Church* by William Sydnor (Wilton, Conn.: Morehouse-Barlow, 1980)
□ *Introduction to the Episcopal Church* by Joseph B. Bernardin (Morehouse, 1992)
□ Episcopal Church Web site: www.ecusa.anglican.org

Table of Comparison	*Episcopalians*	*Lutherans*
Teachings	1. Accept Apostles' and Nicene Creeds. 2. Accept the Bible as the Word of God. 3. Celebrate two sacraments; observe five additional sacramentals. 4. Believe in Christ's real presence in Communion; some explain it as only spiritual, others are close to Roman Catholic view of transubstantiation. 5. Insist on apostolic succession, that is, bishops must be ordained in an unbroken line back to the apostles.	1. Same. 2. Same. 3. Celebrate two sacraments: Baptism and Communion. 4. Believe in Christ's real presence in Communion, that is, communicant receives body and blood of Christ with the bread and wine. 5. Apostolic succession is understood as continuity with the apostles' teaching.
Type of Worship	Liturgical. Form for main service fixed in *Book of Common Prayer* and subject to change by General Convention.	Liturgical from tradition with basic order followed by custom and church statements.
Government	An episcopal form with three ranks of clergy: bishops, priests, and deacons. The government of the Episcopal Church is democratic, and congregations have considerable freedom.	Interdependent congregational, regional, national, and global expressions of the church characterized by democratic decision making, strong ecumenical relationships, elected leadership, and an ordained ministry.
Characteristics	Great appeal to upper- and middle-class people, although it attracts all classes and races.	Strongest appeal among the middle class, although not exclusively so.
Statistics*	Membership . . . . 2,536,550 Congregations . . . . 7,415 *U. S. statistics from *Yearbook of American and Canadian Churches 1998.*	

CHAPTER 13

Evangelical Covenant Church

The Evangelical Covenant Church accepts the Old and New Testaments as the Word of God and the only perfect rule for faith, doctrine, and conduct.

Within the relatively formal Swedish Lutheran church in the nineteenth century, movements sprang up that called for a personal experience of grace. These movements, combined with aspects of English Evangelicalism, had significant influence upon the life of a young Uppsala University student, Carl Olof Rosenius. This influence would bear fruit as Rosenius became the leader of the evangelical movement in Sweden.

Mission Friends

It was within the evangelical movement that the Mission Covenant of Sweden was born in 1878. This was a *free church,* since it was not a part of the Lutheran State Church of Sweden.

Mission Covenant beliefs were carried to the United States by young immigrants. In this country many of them affiliated with the Augustana Lutheran Church, which eventually became part of the ELCA. But when these "Mission Friends" felt that too many church members gave little evidence of new life in Christ, they began to seek fellowship elsewhere. Congregationalists sought to gain their participation; various synodical ventures, such as the Mission and Ansgar Synods, were attempted. But in February 1885, the "Mission Friends" organized the Evangelical Covenant Church of America. Here was a body of people who emphasized life above doctrine, a congregational polity, a free liturgy, and an insistence on evidence of new life. They have had a great interest in evangelism and missions.

Today, the Covenant church has taken its place among the smaller, but vital, denominations of American Protestantism. Its active concern for Christian education and nurture, evangelism and outreach, missions and social responsibility, mark it as a church concerned to be relevant in today's world. The problems of Covenanters are the problems of Christians—how to translate the heritage of faith into meaningful terms so that it can touch the lives of people from many different ethnic backgrounds.

While the Covenant church does not belong to either the World Council of Churches or the National Council of Churches, it does cooperate with several of their agencies. Some of its members have participated in significant places of leadership.

Conservative in Theology

The Evangelical Covenant Church represents in general the theologically conservative and evangelical heritage within Protestantism. It accepts the Holy Scriptures, the Old and the New Testaments, as the Word of God and the only perfect rule for faith, doctrine, and conduct. It values the historic confessions of the Christian church, particularly the Apostles' Creed; however, it has not made subscription to a particular creed a requirement for membership in the church.

The Covenant church follows the classical trinitarian beliefs. God's love and mercy are fully revealed in Jesus Christ. Jesus Christ shared our human situation, experienced our anguish, despair, alienation, guilt, and condemnation. Through Christ's death and resurrection, God cancelled the power of sin and released us from its bondage. The atonement is for all people, but its benefits are known only to those who participate in faith.

Human beings were created in God's image for fellowship with God. Created as a free moral agent, humankind has now fallen into sin through its own deliberate choice. Original sin holds the human race in a bondage from which it cannot, through its own will, extricate itself. Our sin is essentially our desire to manage our lives on our own terms without calling upon God. Salvation becomes a reality only when we confess our sin, admit our inability to save ourselves, and wholeheartedly place our trust in the grace of God. We are justified, not by our works, but solely by faith, which is itself made possible through the grace of God.

Gathered Church

The Covenant church holds to the ideal of the *gathered* or *believers* church. The basic requirement for membership is personal acceptance of Christ as Savior and Lord and a life that is not in contradiction to that confession. The denomination does not ask for ethnic, cultural, or economic uniformity, or for doctrinal uniformity in matters that are not central to the faith. Members must, however, hold themselves subject to the authority of Scripture.

Baptism and Holy Communion are divinely ordained sacraments. While the Covenant church has traditionally practiced the baptism of infants, it holds within its fellowship both those who accept adult baptism and those who accept infant baptism. It requires that its ministers recognize the validity of infant as well as adult baptism and administer either form when so requested.

Worship is dignified, but without elaborate liturgy. Emphasis falls upon the faithful preaching of the Word in the conviction that the entire life and thought of God's people must be shaped by the living Word. Music, also, has played a large role in Covenant worship.

The priesthood of all believers doctrine is given a central place. Christ's ministry is carried on through the church as a whole, and every member shares in responsibility for witness to the gospel. This ministry includes concern for the physical and social needs of people as well as the spiritual. The purpose of both the social and spiritual concern is to bring others to acceptance of Christ and to glorify God through realizing God's will in the world.

For Discussion

□ What signs do you see that point to the Covenant church's origins within the Lutheran church?
□ What points of difference do you see between the two?
□ How important do you think it is that each church member's life give evidence of their faith?

For Further Study

□ Available through Covenant Church offices:
□ *Covenant Affirmations* (pamphlet and book) by Donald Frisk (Chicago: Covenant Publications, 1988)
□ *A Precious Heritage* by Philip Anderson (Northwest Conference, Covenant Church, 1984)
□ *By One Spirit* by Karl Olson (Chicago: Covenant Press, 1962)
□ Covenant church Web site: www.covchurch.org

Table of Comparison	*Covenant*	*Lutherans*
Teachings	1. Accept the Bible as the Word of God.	1. Accept the Bible as the written witness to God's revelation through Jesus Christ.
	2. Believe in the triune nature of God.	2. Same.
	3. Believe in full divinity and humanity of Christ.	3. Same.
	4. Teach justification by grace through faith.	4. Same.
	5. Practice a gathered church.	5. See the church called by the gospel through Word and sacrament.
	6. Accept Baptism and Holy Communion as sacraments. Either adult or infant baptism may be practiced, but infant form traditional.	6. Celebrate sacraments of Baptism and Holy Communion. Unbaptized adults are baptized, but infant baptism is regular practice.
Type of Worship	Dignified but without elaborate liturgy. Emphasis on preaching of the Word.	Liturgical patterns utilized with emphasis on both preaching of the Word and celebration of the sacraments.
Government	Member congregations support policies and programs of the Covenant Church while maintaining broad freedom in local matters.	Interdependent congregational, regional, national, and global expressions of the church characterized by democratic decision making, strong ecumenical relationships, elected leadership, and an ordained ministry.
Characteristics	Emphasis on new life in Christ and its expression in modern life. Not a member of, but cooperates with, WCC and NCC.	Emphasis on justification by grace through faith with call to make faith active in life. Member of NCC and WCC.
Statistics*	Membership . . . . 93,136 Congregations . . . . 615 *U. S. statistics from *Yearbook of American and Canadian Churches 1998.*	

CHAPTER 14

Evangelical Free Church

Worship in the Evangelical Free Church is orderly without being extremely formal. Singing is sometimes led by a praise team.

Freedom has been a question of considerable importance for many people in the history of the Christian church. Some wanted freedom to interpret the Bible as they pleased. Others sought freedom from ecclesiastical or civil authority. Such a concern for freedom was evident among many immigrants. For some, it was the main motivation for coming to America. It is not surprising that many of these immigrants established churches which were *free* from all organizational ties. In this way, they hoped to have the freedom they sought.

Free Churches

Scandinavian immigrants were already acquainted with a "free church" concept. Groups of people had meetings separate from the state churches for a number of years. Once on American soil, these immigrants continued these *free* meetings with only a minimum amount of organization.

During the early part of the twentieth century, there were enough *free* congregations that two national organizations were formed for fellowship. The Swedish Evangelical Free Church of the United States of America was incorporated in 1908, and the Norwegian-Danish Evangelical Free Church Association of North America was officially formed in 1912. These two organizations merged in 1950 to form the Evangelical Free Church of America.

Worship and Practice

Qualification for church membership is based on the evidence of conversion and the living of the Christian life.

There is no single pattern of worship within the local congregations. The services generally involve the singing of hymns, the reading of scripture, and a sermon preached by the congregation's minister. These services are orderly without being extremely formal. The amount of formality varies from church to church.

Two ordinances are practiced: the Lord's supper and baptism. The Free church follows the tradition of Zwingli rather than Luther concerning the Lord's supper.

It believes that Christ is present in the Communion service only in a spiritual sense, and not in a real way.

Baptism is considered to be a demonstration to the world that salvation has taken place. It is not seen as a means of salvation. Both immersion and sprinkling are permitted within the framework of the statement of faith. At the present time, more congregations practice immersion than sprinkling.

The Evangelical Free Church takes a strong stand on the authority of the Bible. It believes that the scriptures, including both the Old and New Testaments, are the inspired Word of God, without error in the original writings.

In all doctrine and church organization, the denomination seeks to follow its best interpretations of the Scriptures. These beliefs are summarized in a 12-article statement that was adopted in 1950 at the time of the merger. Major points in that statement of faith include an affirmation of the triune nature of God as Father, Son, and Holy Spirit. Also confessed in the statement is the fallen, sinful condition of humanity. In this lost condition, eternal life is obtained only through regeneration by the Holy Spirit. Although salvation is made possible by the death of Christ, it must be taken by each individual through a personal belief in Jesus and the acceptance of him as Savior.

Organization for Fellowship

The local churches have a congregational form of government. They have the right to govern their own affairs without interference from the denomination. The local church calls its own pastor who has been prepared through training and ordination to minister to the spiritual needs of the people.

The local free churches are united into the Evangelical Free Church of America. According to the Articles of Incorporation, this is done "for such mutual activities beyond the scope and ability of a local congregation." At the same time, it is declared that the Evangelical Free Church organization has "no controlling power over the internal affairs" of the cooperating congregations. The national organization is meant for fellowship and cooperative work, not for any centralizing of authority.

Social Attitudes

Although the denomination believes that Christians should be concerned about the problems that face society, direct social action has never been a major thrust. It does have a Committee on Social Concern which makes recommendations to the general conference concerning involvement in social problems.

Much of the denomination's ministry of social action is done through cooperative effort with several other denominations in the National Association of Evangelicals.

For Discussion

□ Why do you think a "free church" might have been attractive to immigrants?
□ How does an Evangelical Free Church congregation's complete freedom compare with the way your church body is organized?
□ Talk about the idea of the Bible being without error in the original writings.

For Further Study

□ Evangelical Free Church Web site: www.efca.org

Table of Comparison	*Free Church*	*Lutherans*
Teachings	1. Believe the Bible is the Word of God. 2. Believe in the triune nature of God. 3. Believe in full divinity and full humanity of Christ. 4. Teach justification by faith. 5. Consider baptism and Holy Communion as symbols. 6. Presence of Christ in Holy Communion affirmed only in a spiritual sense.	1. Believe the Bible is the written witness to God's revelation of saving action through Jesus Christ. 2. Same. 3. Same. 4. Teach justification by grace through faith. 5. Celebrate sacraments of Baptism and Holy Communion as means of God's grace. 6. Real presence of Christ in Holy Communion accepted.
Type of Worship	Somewhat informal with no stated liturgy.	Liturgical, following primary patterns of Western church.
Government Characteristics	Congregational form with each local church in complete control of its own affairs.	Interdependent congregational, regional, national, and global expressions of the church characterized by democratic decision making, strong ecumenical relationships, elected leadership, and an ordained ministry.
	Strong stand on authority of the Bible, but view baptism and communion as ordinances and symbols.	Emphasis on the Word and the sacraments of Baptism and Communion. Bible considered basic authority for faith and life.
Statistics*	Membership . . . . 242,619 Congregations . . . . 1,224 *U. S. statistics from *Yearbook of American and Canadian Churches 1998.*	

CHAPTER 15

Evangelical Lutheran Church in America

Martin Luther nailed his "Ninety-five Theses" on the door of the Wittenberg Castle Church on October 31, 1517.

For many who are using this book, *Lutheran* would describe not "our neighbor's faith" but our own. Still, in the context of all these churches and denominations, it is helpful to look again at what we believe and how the Lutheran church came to be what it is. That is what this chapter is about.

The Reformation of the sixteenth century divided the church in Europe. Yet this division was not Martin Luther's original purpose; he only wanted to reform and renew the existing church. He did not want to begin a separate denomination of Christians, much less a church that bears his name. Luther's sole concern was proper biblical teaching for the "one, holy, catholic, and apostolic" church. Unfortunately, this concern led Luther and other reformers into conflict with the teachings of the Roman church of the time. The resulting body, the Lutheran church, is both protestant and catholic.

Radical Focus on Grace

If you were to boil down Lutheran beliefs to one word, a strong candidate for that word would be *grace*. Lutherans teach that we are who we are because of God's grace—that is, God's love for us without our deserving it in any way. This grace is shown in countless ways, but most clearly of all in the good news that we are saved only through the death and resurrection of Jesus Christ. That is the gospel, the kernel of our life and hope, and all else is secondary to this.

Most—if not all—Christian churches also point to God's grace, but Lutherans tend to get really radical about it. They say that anything that is added to the gospel of Jesus Christ as a source of life or requirement for living is misguided. It may be well-meaning, even beneficial, but it must not be put on the same level as the gospel. If these things are put on the same level as the gospel, that is when Lutherans often find themselves in the "reformation" mode.

So, for instance, are Christians called upon to rely on the gospel *and* other traditional teachings? Such traditions can be helpful, but if they don't have biblical support, Lutherans would say that we cannot be bound to them. At the same time, Lutherans have tried to hold to as much of the larger, "catholic" church as they can—as long as it doesn't conflict with the gospel. Lutheran worship is usually built on the classical Western-church pattern, but that is not required.

Are Christians called upon to be "born again" or live in a certain way as evidence of their faith—and perhaps only then be baptized? In this case, it is a lifestyle that has been added to the gospel. Of course Christians will want to live good, moral lives, but we are not saved by what we do, only by God's free grace given to sinners and even infants.

Justification by Grace through Faith

While Lutherans agree with all Christians that faith involves personal commitment and that it is meant to result in a life lived for others, they shy away from using these actions to decide whether a person really has faith. After all, we have all had times when we fail to do the right thing. These times, according to Lutheran teaching, reveal what kind of persons we really are by stripping away illusions and pride. We learn about our weakness, vulnerability, and the depth of sin. We begin to know how much we need the mercy and understanding of others. At such times we may be particularly open to the message of the gospel, because the gospel tells us that God accepts people despite their failed commitments.

Lutherans see this acceptance in spite of our failures and sin as the heart of the teaching of Jesus. We see it in Bible passages such as the parable of the prodigal son. The gospel teaches that God forgives us even though we have failed. Because Jesus died on the cross for us, God receives us. All we need to do is turn to God in our troubled times. We have a place to go, and God rejoices in our homecoming.

No one—no matter how good—can ever earn his or her own salvation. The Law found in the Bible convinces us that all have fallen short of God's demands. That is why the gospel is so central to our faith: our only source of hope is its assurance of God's grace to the ungodly through Jesus Christ. This teaching Lutherans call "justification by grace through faith alone."

The Word of God

Lutherans hold a number of teachings in common with the vast majority of other Christian denominations. One of the most important teachings concerns the understanding of the Word of God. Lutherans commonly speak of the Word of God in three senses.

First, the Word of God is Jesus Christ himself who was "In the beginning . . . with God" and indeed "was God" (John 1:1). This same Word "became flesh and lived among us" (John 1:14).

Second, the Word of God is the message about Jesus Christ, his life, death, and resurrection, which is the subject of the New Testament and the subject to which the Old Testament points as it tells of God's work of salvation among the people of Israel. In this sense, the "Word of God" means the same as the "gospel"—the good news of Jesus Christ that is proclaimed by believers (see 1 Peter 1:24–25). This sense of the Word of God, coming out of the meaning of scripture itself, protects Lutherans from the danger of worshiping the Bible. God's Word is good news that cannot be imprisoned in black type. It must be proclaimed in every generation with a living voice.

Third, however, Lutherans affirm that the Word of God is the whole Bible, Old and New Testaments. The Bible ensures the accuracy and fidelity of the church to the gospel. It protects the people of God from false teaching and tells them the rich and varied story of God's work of salvation. The Bible is the record of divine revelation. It is the final authority for all preaching and teaching. No doctrine or tradition of the church overrules it or adds to it. The Reformation had an appropriate slogan: *sola scriptura*—Scripture alone!

The Means of Grace

Lutherans celebrate the sacraments of Baptism and the Lord's Supper. (Some, based on the Lutheran Confessions, also consider confession and absolution to be a sacrament.) Sacraments are specific, external signs that convey God's grace and mercy instituted by Christ himself. The sacraments use the common elements of water, bread, and wine transformed by the Word of God into means of salvation.

Baptism is the entryway into the church. Following ancient Christian practice, Lutherans baptize infants, an action that is in line with their belief that we are saved by God's grace, not by anything we could possibly do. Baptism begins the journey of faith, yet it is to be acknowledged daily in the Christian life.

Christ also instituted the Lord's Supper "on the night when he was betrayed" (1 Corinthians 11:23). The Lord's Supper is the true body and blood of Christ given in sacrifice for us beginning on that night long ago. It nourishes the believer throughout life, assuring the believer of forgiveness from sin and of the presence of God in what is often a dark and hostile world.

Preaching the gospel and sharing the sacraments are, according to Lutheran teaching, the work of the church. Where these are performed, there the church is to be found. This definition of the church is truly ecumenical. The church does not need a certain sign on the door. It does not need a specific form of church government. The church is the Word of God, the sacraments of Baptism and the Lord's Supper, and sinners seeking God's grace. Where these are found, there the church lives. That is also why coming together in worship is so important for Lutherans—that is where we hear the Word preached and receive the sacraments.

Christian Service: Faith Active in Love

Finally, Lutherans know with all Christians that true faith is active in love for our neighbor. As Jesus sought the outcast and outsider in his ministry, so the church seeks them in its ministry. The church is called to serve people in material as well as spiritual needs. The reason for involvement is the ministry of all Christian people: "Truly I tell you, just as you did it to one of the least of these who are members of my family, you did it to me" (Matthew 25:40).

The Lutheran Landscape

Most of what has been said regarding Lutheran beliefs applies to all Lutherans; however, as is true of many families of churches, Lutherans are divided. Some of these divisions are due to ethnic reasons: people from different areas had different languages and varying national allegiances that carried over as some immigrated to America. Other divisions have to do with disagreements over doctrine and church practice. Splits have occurred over matters as diverse as whether it is proper to take out insurance, how much authority the church headquarters should have, and whether women should be ordained into the ministry.

The two largest Lutheran denominations in the United States are the Evangelical Lutheran Church in America (ELCA) and The Lutheran Church—Missouri Synod (LCMS). The ELCA is the larger of the two, and is the publisher of this book. The LCMS is considered in its own chapter on page 83. Besides these two, the Wisconsin Evangelical Lutheran Synod (WELS) has about 400,000 members, and there are a number of other, very small groups.

In a book that shows the many divisions within Christianity, it is refreshing to report that the ELCA is the result of a long line of mergers. Most of the Lutheran bodies that eventually formed the ELCA came from German, Norwegian, and Swedish roots, though other nationalities are also represented. The ELCA was formed in 1987 in the merger of three Lutheran denominations, the American Lutheran Church (itself a product of four groups with Norwegian, German, and Danish roots), the Lutheran Church in America (which came out of backgrounds including Swedish, German, Danish, Finnish, and Slovak), and the small Association of Evangelical Lutheran Churches (which separated from the LCMS in the 1970s).

The Evangelical Lutheran Church in America tends toward the middle in the spectrum of American Christianity, regarding both doctrine and social issues. It joins with most mainline Protestant churches in supporting the ordination of women to the ministry. It looks to the Bible for authority in its preaching and teaching, yet does not take a literalist approach to scripture. It has found it necessary to wrestle with thorny social issues, but its positions are neither wildly liberal nor rigidly conservative. Ecumenically, it has been an enthusiastic partner in dialogues with other churches, and where possible without compromising its beliefs, it has entered into fellowship with them. Growing from deep, strong roots, it enters the twenty-first century equipped for and intent upon reaching out with the good news of Jesus Christ.

For Discussion

□ What would you consider the strongest aspects of the Lutheran church? The weakest?

□ If you are a member of an ELCA congregation that is older than the ELCA (that is, begun before 1987), what are its historical roots?

□ Why do you belong to the denomination you are a member of? That is, why this one, and not another?

For Further Study

□ *Martin Luther: Exploring His Life and Times, 1483–1546.* Multi-media CD-ROM by Helmar Junghans (Minneapolis: Augsburg Fortress, 1998)

□ *The Book of Concord* (the "confessions" that define Lutheran beliefs) ed. Theodore G. Tappert (Philadelphia: Fortress Press, 1959)

□ *The Lutheran People* pamphlet by Martin E. Marty (Madison Heights, Mich.: Cathedral Directories, rev. 1989)

□ Evangelical Lutheran Church in America web site: www.elca.org

---

Evangelical Lutheran Church in America

Statistics*

Membership	5,180,910
Congregations	10,936

*U. S. statistics from *Yearbook of American and Canadian Churches 1998.*

CHAPTER 16

Hinduism (Vedanta)

A worshiper remembers and honors Brahman by lighting incense before the image of a Hindu deity.

"Truth is one—sages call it by various names" (*Rig Veda*).

The religion known to most Westerners as Hinduism encompasses many different spiritual practices. These religious sects are unified by their reliance on ancient texts called the Vedas as the primary source of inspiration and the basis for philosophy and spiritual practice. The Vedas are considered to be timeless truths revealed to anonymous sages at least four to five thousand years ago. *Veda* means "knowledge" in Sanskrit.

The primary philosophy based on the Vedas is called *Vedanta,* literally meaning "the culmination of the Vedas." There are four Vedas, each with four parts. The last and most philosophical portion of each Veda contains the Upanishads. It is upon these climactic texts known as the Upanishads that the Vedantic philosophy of Hinduism is based.

The three main schools of Vedanta philosophy are categorized according to whether God (Brahman) and humanity are understood as separate (dualism); humanity is the parts, God is the whole (qualified non-dualism); or God and humanity are united (non-dualism or *Advaita*). Each of these schools attempts to address the universal and timeless mystery: the relationship between God, humankind, and nature. The easiest way to explain the various schools of thought as well as the practice of different sects is to start with Advaita Vedanta as taught by Shankara, philosopher-saint of the seventh century.

The Nature of Brahman and the Universe

Use of the term *Brahman* is common to all schools of Vedanta. It is used in much the same way that "God" is used in Christianity. It is employed to refer to the highest, most exalted entity to be known—the Absolute. According to Vedanta philosophy, the goal of life is to establish a pure and eternal relationship with this ultimate reality.

Brahman is beyond words. It is the one ultimate reality. The best we can do is to say what it is not. Brahman is that *infinite* (not subject to boundaries), *undivided, unchanging* reality. The positive qualities that best point to Brahman are absolute *existence,* absolute *consciousness,* and absolute *bliss.*

In Hindu thought, this universe is a misperception of that one reality. All that we see and experience merely appears to be real. The power of Brahman to project this apparent reality is known as maya. This apparent reality is nothing but the play of pure consciousness that forms what seems to be our universe.

The Nature of Human Beings

Our true nature is divine, one with Brahman. We fail to realize our own divine nature because we believe what our senses tell us. They take in what seems to be a finite, divided, changing universe in space and time with laws of causation, and we assume that that is reality. Our genetic programming, as well as our scientific worldview, make us identify with our body and mind. We feel finite, separated from the rest of the universe, and subject to change, disease, death.

The goal of life, as understood by Hinduism, is to see through our mistake and realize our true nature. As seen within the context of the illusion of space and time, we are individual souls—*jivas*—seeking to be reunited with that absolute Brahman. In the context of the individual, that absolute Brahman is called the *Atman.*

Karma and Reincarnation

Within this world of time, space, and causation, things appear to work in certain ways. The laws of physics tell us that for every action there is a reaction. Every one of our actions, thoughts, and desires creates a kind of vibrational impression (*samskara*) on us. These samskaras are what give us our tendencies. The law of karma states that until one transcends this relative plane of existence and is reunited with Brahman, every action will have its reaction. Our karma (actions) may not bear fruit in this life, but may be stored until a future life. At the time of death, if an individual has not yet realized his or her divine nature, the soul (*jiva*) after death may experience heavenly or hellish realms until he or she reincarnates in a new body. The options available to the jiva are restricted according to the stored karmas and the lessons that need to be learned.

Ways of Thinking about This World

Because, as we have said, the world is a misperception of the reality, there is uncertainty about it. To illustrate, if you mistakenly think a rope is a snake, you will always be uncertain about what species of snake it is. You will be trying to analyze it in terms of snakes, not of ropes. Similarly, in terms of the world, we can never fully understand the nature of Brahman. Once we realize Brahman as our true nature, we will have no uncertainty—but we will still not be able to accurately describe it in words. Once you realize the rope is not a snake, you will know it as a rope, but you still cannot accurately describe it in snake terminology.

This apparent universe of ours can be thought of as the dream of Brahman who has projected this universe and entered into it, just as we enter a dream world when we sleep. Our dream world often has little reality compared to our waking state. We project the dream and enter into it. Similarly, our perception of this world has no reality when compared to the realization of God.

Why do we misperceive Brahman (God) to be this world of duality? From within maya (the illusory world), there is no answer. Beyond maya (in the true existence with Brahman), the question does not arise. The closest thing to an understanding we can have is to say that God "creates" the world as a divine play (*lila*).

Duality, Gods, and Goddesses

When the One appears manifest as many, it must do so in pairs of opposites. The dividing of everything with names and forms is also a major characteristic of this cosmic dream.

We can think of Brahman as being like a stringed instrument. Music is like the creation. The vibrations of the sound occur equally in both directions, as pairs of opposites. The various levels of existence from the gross world to such subtle levels as our mental plane, or heavenly planes of existence, are like octaves of each other.

The male-female duality is sometimes used to symbolize and personify the active and inactive aspects of the absolute Brahman. The active principle is the feminine: the Divine Mother. The Divine Mother is Brahman's power to manifest, to create the cosmic illusion—maya—of the many out of the one. Hinduism also uses three god/goddess pairs to personify the three aspects of the manifest world: creation, preservation, and destruction. Other sects see all three aspects in one deity. It is important to remember that all the various gods and goddesses of Hinduism are but aspects of Brahman (the absolute one God) as seen through maya.

An Incarnation is the highest manifestation of God in living human form. Generally both male and female aspects are represented. The major examples are Rama/Sita, Krishna/Radha, Buddha/Jasodhara, Christ/Virgin Mary (as Hindus would understand them), and Ramakrishna/Holy Mother.

Waking Up through Spiritual Practices

Since our true nature is really infinite, undivided, and unchanging, we naturally seek to find those qualities within this world. Our yearning for freedom, love, and peace in this world can be seen as our attempt at discovering, respectively, our true infinite, undivided, and unchanging nature. But in the world, the more you get of one, the less you have of one of the other two. It is only through spiritual practices that one can "wake up" to his or her true nature and find absolute freedom, love, and peace. In Hinduism it is recognized that all the various religious paths can lead one to God. All the seeming contradictions disappear when the goal is realized. Only pure peace, pure love, and pure freedom remain.

There are many ways we can help ourselves to wake up to our true nature. Here is some general advice.

- Remember that your true nature is divine, that some day, eventually, you will reach the goal.
- Accept yourself where you are and go forward from there.
- Choose the path that best fits your temperament and your natural inclinations. Give your activities a spiritual turn. Figure out ways you can best remember God.
- The goal is to realize your oneness with God. The two main obstacles are forgetting that the world is God in disguise and thus being distracted by your senses, and letting your ego think you are separate and different from others.

Hinduism recognizes specific forms of spiritual practices (*yogas*) for realizing our true nature. Four of these yogas are

- *Karma Yoga*—the path of selfless action. Do your work with the attitude of unselfishness and detachment from the results. Do not expect to make the world perfect. See and serve the Divine in other beings.
- *Jnana Yoga*—affirm your true nature. Say, "I am not the mind. I am not the body. I am pure existence, pure consciousness, pure bliss."
- *Bhakti Yoga*—develop a loving relationship with a personal aspect of God. Choose a deity (god or goddess) or an incarnation of God. Relate everything in your life to the chosen deity. Perform a ceremony (sacrament) called a *puja* or worship. The puja is designed to give the worshiper the aid of physical objects and actions to keep the worshiper's mind on the chosen form of God. This chosen form is treated like an honored guest with various symbolic offerings.

□ *Raja Yoga*—gaining control over the mind. This is done through meditation, calming the mind to get a clear view of its true nature. Repetition of sacred words or mantras and breath control help to amplify the spiritual vibrations.

Classifying Various Hindu Beliefs

This chapter has been describing Advaita, or non-dualist, Hinduism. The two other main schools of Vedanta philosophy are qualified non-dualism (where rather than thinking that you are one with God, you are a part of God like a spark from the fire) and dualism (where you and God are separate and the goal is to be eternally in God's presence).

Sometimes Hinduism is divided into groups depending on which deity is the primary focus of worship. All deities are accepted as manifestations of the one Brahman, but different groups take different deities as the highest manifestation or the most efficacious to worship. Each is like a different doorway to reach the one Brahman. For example, Shaivites worship Shiva; Vaishnavas worship incarnations of Vishnu (also known as Rama or Krishna); and Shaktas worship a form of the Divine Mother, such as Durga or Kali.

Tantra is another Advaitic (non-dual) philosophy. Whereas Shankara's Advaita Vedanta emphasizes the unreality of the world compared with Brahman, Tantra emphasizes that this world is nothing but Shakti, the power of Brahman, that this world is Brahman in disguise to be worshiped as the Divine Mother. Our consciousness should be trained to see Shakti or the Divine Mother in everything, to use everything as a reminder of the all-pervading oneness. All the yogas can still be followed with slight changes in attitude.

Organizations and Hinduism

Hinduism is not centrally organized. It did *not* start with one person or group, with one church from which others broke away. Many temples are independent entities where people come to worship. Traditionally, study of the scriptures was done by independent teachers (gurus) who had experienced God in a transcendental way, some of whom would give initiation into certain spiritual practices. It was primarily one group of Hindus, the Brahmin caste of India, that was responsible for learning the scriptures. Most homes would have a family shrine where their chosen deity would be worshiped every day.

Today, in addition to independent temples, there are organizations with branch centers throughout India and the world, the Ramakrishna Order being one of the largest. It is inspired by Sri Ramakrishna (1836–1886) who lived in Bengal, India. He followed all paths described above as well as Christian and Islamic traditions and realized the same oneness with God through each, proving that the same goal can be reached by various paths.

Swami Vivekananda (1863–1902), a disciple of Sri Ramakrishna, was a representative at the first World Parliament of Religions in Chicago in 1893 and the first Hindu to lecture extensively in the West. There are now 15 centers in the U. S. headed by swamis of the Ramakrishna Order founded by Swami Vivekananda.

Today there are many groups representing different aspects of Hinduism. Chinmaya Mission, Self Realization Fellowship, Shivananda Yoga, International Society of Krishna Consciousness, Siddha Yoga, as well as many other groups and independent gurus teach in the United States. As more Indians come to live in this country, individual Hindu temples are being built.

Because Hinduism accepts all traditions as valid approaches to God, most Hindu groups have no missionary zeal, no need to convert others. But because of its all-encompassing nature, Vedanta philosophy is adaptable to any culture and country and is being studied and accepted by many Westerners. The influence of Vedantic ideas can be seen in groups not classified as Hindu. Hindus believe that by studying different religions they can come to a deeper understanding of their own, and hope that studying Hinduism will do the same for you.

For Discussion

□ Have you had any exposure to Hindu people or beliefs? How have these influenced your opinion of Hinduism?
□ Compare the Hindu understanding of Brahman as being the only reality with the Christian belief in a separate, sovereign God. How might this difference affect how you look at life?
□ Look at the descriptions of the four yogas. Could some of these be useful for Christians? Could some of them work against our beliefs? How or why?

For Further Study

□ *The Essentials of Hinduism* by Swami Bhaskarananda (Seattle: Viveka Press, 1994)
□ *The Upanishads,* translated by Swami Prabhavananda and Fredrick Manchester (Vedanta Press, 1996)
□ *The Bhagavad-Gita, The Song of God,* translated by Swami Prabhavananda and Christopher Isherwood (New American Library, 1993)
□ Web site: www.vedanta.org

Table of Comparison	*Advaita Vedanta*	*Lutherans*
Teachings	1. Understand Brahman as the Absolute; however, Brahman is seen as various manifestations, such as Rama/Sita and Krishna/Radha.	1. Believe in a personal, triune God—Father, Son, Holy Spirit. These persons remain unchanged through eternity.
	2. Our universe is an illusion, a misperception of the one reality that is Brahman.	2. All things are created by God and are subject to God. God is separate from creation, which includes humans.
	3. Our goal in life is to realize that we are one with Brahman.	3. We are alienated from God, but through Christ's death, we are saved and brought back to God.
	4. Hindus believe in karma, the law of cause and effect.	4. Though humans have the freedom to disobey God, all is under the umbrella of God's law and grace.
	5. The path to realizing our oneness with Brahman may take many lifetimes, in which we may take many forms.	5. We are created as unique humans, and we each have one earthly life.
Type of Worship	Meditation, repetition of mantras or holy words. Remembering and honoring Brahman with offerings of flowers, food, and incense.	Liturgical from tradition with basic order followed by custom and church statements.
Government	No overall government. Generally, spiritual direction by the head of the local Center, often with elected board of directors.	Interdependent congregational, regional, national, and global expressions of the church characterized by democratic decision making, strong ecumenical relationships, elected leadership, and an ordained ministry.
Characteristics	Mixture of first- and second-generation Indian-Americans, and other Americans from many backgrounds. Tend to be well-educated.	Strongest appeal among the middle class, although not exclusively so.
Statistics*	Membership .... 1,285,000 *Estimated U. S. statistics from *The World Almanac 1999.*	

CHAPTER 17

Islam

Prayer (salah) *is a pillar of the Islam faith and is performed at least five times a day.*

Islam is the religion of choice for one-fifth of the world's population; the number of people who follow it is believed to be second only to Christianity. The Muslim objective is to live for the pleasure of ALLAH, who created humankind to serve HIM only, in order to reach the ultimate goal of Paradise in the next life.

It might be helpful to explain a few things here at the beginning. You will notice that whenever ALLAH or another name for GOD is mentioned, it is in capital letters. This indicates reverence for the holy name, and is traditional in Muslim circles. Then, to clarify terms, it should be pointed out that *Islam* is the name of the religion; the term means "peace" or "submission" in Arabic. If one is referring to one who practices Islam, the term is *Muslim.* (Moslem is an older, less correct spelling.) Finally, you will notice "(*saw*)" whenever the founder of Islam is mentioned. This is an abbreviation for *Sallallahu alayhi wassalam,* Arabic for "May ALLAH's peace and blessings be upon him," and is a statement of respect bestowed upon the Prophet Mohammed (also spelled Muhammad) whenever his name is mentioned.

Seeing Muslims or Muslim events in our neighborhoods or on TV has become commonplace. Unfortunately, the sudden recognition of Muslims coupled with the scarcity of literature on Islam and Muslims has confused many and contributed to misunderstanding, bias, and fear.

Islam arrived in North America early on. The customs of slaves in the 1700s can be traced back to their Islamic heritage. Arabs who came to the United States in the early 1900s practiced their Islamic heritage within the confines of their homes, and so Islam was not as visible in the general community. However, media brought Islam notoriety (for better or worse) through coverage of Nobel Drew Ali (Marcus Garvey or Elijah Muhammad), Malcolm X, the Gulf War, and many other people and events.

More than 40 countries around the world have Muslim populations. Indonesia has the largest concentration, followed by Pakistan, India, and Bangladesh. Islam can be found in places as far-flung as Asia, Africa, the Pacific, and Europe. In the United States, Islam is commonly considered the fastest growing religion. The nation has six to eight million Muslims, including immigrants, recent converts, and first and second generation Muslim Americans.

Source of Muslim Beliefs

Islam is based upon the teachings of Mohammed ibn Abdullah, who lived around 570–632. When Mohammed (*saw*) was 40 years old, he received his first revelation from ALLAH, thus beginning his prophethood. Whenever he received revelation, he recited it to his followers who memorized and wrote down every word. Over a period of 23 years, ALLAH's revelations through the Archangel Gabriel to Prophet Mohammed (*saw*) were collected and became the Holy Qur'an (sometimes spelled Koran). The collected revelation appeals to reason and serves as a guide and warning to all humankind. In it that which is lawful and unlawful, the resulting rewards and punishments, and the criteria for justice are clearly outlined.

Muslims implement, to the best of their ability, the lifestyle contained in the Qur'an and the traditions and sayings of the Prophet Mohammed (*saw*). They hold to the Pillars of Islam, the foundation and strength for their faith:

- Faith (*iman*)—testimonial of ALLAH's Oneness: "There is none worthy of worship except God and Muhammad is the messenger of God."
- Prayer (*salah*)—performed at least five times a day;
- Charity (*zakah*)—setting aside money for those in need;
- Fasting (*sawm*)—during the month of Ramadan;
- Pilgrimage (*hajj*)—to Mecca, required of all who are able, once in their life.

It is worth pointing out that Muslims do not consider Islam to be a religion in the sense of something separate from the rest of life, rather, Islam is for them a complete system of life, encompassing all of existence, including physical, mental, social, spiritual, and academic aspects.

Also noteworthy is that although congregational prayer service (or *Jumuah*) is conducted every Friday at every *Masjid*, or mosque, no special day of worship or sabbath is recognized in Islam. The Muslim prays five obligatory prayers daily, as well as numerous voluntary prayers, and remains in constant remembrance of ALLAH by reciting his praises. Thus the Muslim makes every day a day of worship.

Beliefs of Muslims

In looking at what Muslims believe, it is important not to be confused by merely cultural traditions and values. As we have seen, Islam is found in many different cultures, and sometimes what we think is characteristic of Islam is actually related instead to that particular culture, such as the Arabic culture. That being said, we may look to the Principles of Faith, which constitute shared, common knowledge among Muslims, resulting in the universal oneness, or brotherhood, of the worldwide Islamic community.

The cornerstone of Islam is that ALLAH is one—this monotheism is the foundation of its creed. Beyond that the Principles of Faith, the beliefs that direct the heart and behavior, are these:

- belief in ALLAH;
- belief in his angels;
- belief in his books;
- belief in his messengers;

□ belief in the day of judgment;
□ belief in life after death;
□ belief in divine preordainment.

Some details may be of particular interest to Christians. For instance, Muslims believe that our life on earth is a temporary trial or test, and that eternal life after death is inevitable. Those for whom, in their conduct of earthly life, the good outweighed the bad will enjoy the Paradise. Those whose bad outweighed the good will suffer the wrath of Hell.

Significant differences arise in comparison to Christian beliefs regarding Jesus and the triune God. Islam teaches that Jesus was

□ created; (Qur'an 3:59—"Verily the likeness of Jesus in ALLAH's sight is the likeness of Adam. He created him from dust, then he said to him Be!—and he was.")
□ Messiah of Israel; (Qur'an 3:49—". . . We will appoint [Jesus] a Messenger to the children of Israel . . . ." Qur'an 5:46—". . . We sent [Jesus] the son of Mary confirming the Torah that had come before him and We gave him the Gospel . . . a guidance and admonition for the pious.")
□ a prophet, not God; (Qur'an 4:171—"O people of the Scriptures [Jews and Christians] do not exceed the limits in your religion, say not of ALLAH aught but the truth. The Messiah Jesus, son of Mary was [no more than] a messenger of ALLAH and his Word, . . . Say not 'Three [Trinity]!' Cease, it is better for you, for the Creator (ALLAH) is the only one God, Glory be to him (far exalted is he) above having a son. To him belongs all that is in the heavens and all that is on earth . . . .")
□ neither crucified nor resurrected; (Qur'an 4:157—". . . but they [the Jews] killed him not, nor crucified him, but the resemblance of Jesus was put over another man [and they killed that man] . . . .")
□ one who will return in the last days. (Qur'an 43:61—"And he [Jesus, son of Mary] shall be a known sign for [the coming of] the Hour [Day of Resurrection].")

In agreement with Judaism and Christianity, Islam teaches that God created humankind, beginning with Adam and Eve. All human beings, at their creation, had imprinted upon their essence the creed of ALLAH's Oneship and Lordship. Islam varies from Christianity, however, in its teaching that humankind is born without sin and with the capacity to be and do good for the pleasure of ALLAH and the benefit of the person's own soul. All people have an equal opportunity to choose, by their words and deeds, eternal life in the Hellfire or in Paradise.

Brief History of Islam

The early years of Islam brought suffering, oppression, abuse, and death for the Muslims. To escape persecution, many sought and received refuge and protection from the Christian king of Ethiopia. Eventually, they migrated to Medina, in present-day Saudi Arabia, where they were received with love and generosity. Islam spread within Arabia and beyond its borders. While centralized in the Near East, it moved up into central Asia and across Northern Africa, eventually crossing the Straits of Gibraltar into Spain.

During the European Dark Ages, Islamic scholars and religious leaders continued to educate themselves through research and study. They excelled in the areas of architecture, education, medicine, economics, science, literature, and the arts. The Muslims built libraries, schools and universities, mosques, and developed exceptional communities. The Renaissance brought European scholars to Islam in search of knowledge and guidance, resulting in the intermingling of the European and Islamic cultures.

This history was often obscured, especially due to the colonizing practices of the European powers after Word War I, yet Islam's contributions to the resurrection of civilized society were phenomenal. Notable works, often unacknowledged, still used today can be found in mathematics, physics, chemistry, medicine, astronomy, the works of Aristotle, and much more.

Islamic Community and Customs

Marriage is a very important institution within Islam; in fact, it is said that "marriage is half of religion." Islam recognizes that the foundation of civilized society begins with the family. Marriage, which is ordained by ALLAH, dignifies society and preserves proper human relations.

Those who live in cities have probably seen Muslim women dressed in distinctive garb. Muslim men and women are commanded to dress modestly in garments that do not reveal their physical attributes. The woman covers her hair because it is the crown of her beauty. Covering it dignifies her, her husband and family, and decreases the attention of men. There is no mandate in the Qur'an or in the life of the Prophet for the covering of the face. However, this is practiced in some cultural traditions.

Like the Jews and Christians, Muslims have certain rules guiding their conduct. These rules teach that Muslims should not

□ worship nor share in worship any deity except ALLAH;
□ murder, attack another, nor be an aggressor;
□ break contracts that have been made;
□ commit adultery or fornication;
□ become intoxicated through use of alcohol, wine, or drugs;
□ gamble nor obtain money through illegal means;
□ lie, steal, or covet;
□ commit sodomy (whether with a male or a female) or be homosexual;
□ eat pork or food made with or cooked in pork, unless forced by necessity;
□ cause fear or discomfort to their neighbor;
□ be immodest, indecent, vulgar, or decadent;
□ spy on, be suspicious of, backbite, slander, or gossip about others;
□ practice discrimination.

Islam recognizes two holidays, observed at varying dates each year according to the lunar calendar. Each celebration begins with congregational prayer, followed by a sermon, and including hearty feasts, gift-giving, visiting family and friends, community festivities, carnivals, and the like. The holidays are *Eidul Fitr,* which celebrates the victory (end) of the obligatory fast of Ramadan, and *Eidul Adha,* which marks the end of the pilgrimage and also recognizes Prophet Abraham's devotion and obedience to ALLAH's command to sacrifice his son. Animals are slaughtered, or sacrificed, and the meat distributed to the poor.

What the Prophet Mohammed (*saw*) said about

□ racism: "All mankind is from Adam and Eve, an Arab has no superiority over a non-Arab; a white has no superiority over a black nor black over white except by piety...."

□ monetary interest: "ALLAH has forbidden you to take interest.... You will neither inflict nor suffer inequity. ALLAH has judged that there shall be no interest...."

□ religion: "No Prophet or Apostle will come after me and no new faith will be born."
□ Satan: "Beware of Satan for the safety of your religion. He has lost all hope of leading you astray in big things, so beware of following him in small things."
□ women: (Qur'an 4:34: "Men are the protectors and maintainers of women, because ALLAH has made the one excel the other in strength and because they spend [to support them] from their means.") "You have certain rights regarding women, but they also have rights over you. Remember that you have taken them as your wives only under ALLAH's trust and with his permission. If they abide by your right, then to them belongs the right to be fed and clothed in kindness. Do treat your women well and be kind to them for they are your partners and committed helpers. And, it is your right that they do not make friends with anyone whom you do not approve as well as never be unchaste."

Definitions

As Islam becomes more widespread, you may come across some unfamiliar terms. Here are a few of those Arabic terms and what they mean.
□ *ALLAH:* The One, the Only—one of the many names of God.
□ *Jihad:* The challenge to achieve piety, submission, and obedience to ALLAH. (Interpretation as a holy war is misleading.)
□ *Ramadan:* Ninth month of the Islamic lunar calendar, observed as a time of fasting. (Nothing is eaten during daylight hours, though children and the sick are exempt.)
□ *Zakah:* Obligatory distribution of wealth. After taking care of the necessities of life, an annual donation of 2.5 percent of wealth is distributed to the poor and needy.
□ *Hajj:* Pilgrimage, specifically a journey to Mecca, Saudi Arabia, to perform ordained rituals seeking ALLAH's forgiveness and mercy. Every physically, mentally, and financially able Muslim should undertake this journey once in a lifetime.
□ *Imam:* The respected title given to the leader of an Islamic community. Any devout and respected Muslim who leads the prayers.

For Discussion

□ Muslims will sometimes refer to believers from three religions—Judaism, Christianity, and Islam—as "people of the Book." Why is that an appropriate title?
□ Islam developed after Christianity. Generally, what is our attitude toward later revelations such as this? What are our criteria to determine what religion is true?
□ In what areas do you think Islam is most misunderstood by the average American?

For Further Study

□ *Focus on Al-Islam. A series of interviews with Imam W. Deen Mohammed.* (Chicago: Zakat Publications, 1988)
□ *Islam: The Straight Path* by John L. Esposito (New York: Oxford, 1988)
□ *Islam: Its Meaning, Objectives, and Legislative System* by Abdullah Muhammad Khouj (1994)

Table of Comparison	*Muslims*	*Lutherans*
Teachings	1. Believe that God (ALLAH) is one.	1. Believe in the triune God—one God, in three persons.
	2. Believe that a number of God's prophets, including Jesus, culminated in the revelations to the Prophet Mohammed.	2. Believe that Jesus is the Son of God, that his life, death, and resurrection completed God's work of our salvation.
	3. See Islam as a total way of life.	3. See themselves as instruments of God in the world, not necessarily separate from it.
	4. Look to the Qur'an (the words of God through Gabriel to Mohammed) as the prime source for faith and practice.	4. Look to the Bible—Old and New Testaments—as the only written Word of God by which we must believe.
	5. Try to live according to the five Pillars of Faith.	5. No comparable framework, but look to teachings such as the Ten Commandments and the Sermon on the Mount.
Type of Worship	Congregational prayer held on Friday, during which men and women form separate lines for prayer, and hear a sermon by the imam.	Liturgical form typically includes hymns, prayers, readings, sermon, and Holy Communion based on ecumenical patterns.
Government	Local Islamic communities led by imams. Explicit rules in Qur'an guide community life.	Interdependent congregational, regional, national, and global expressions of the church characterized by democratic decision making, strong ecumenical relationships, elected leadership, and an ordained ministry.
Characteristics	Islam provides much of the believers' identity. Family-oriented, strong sense of community. Education is highly valued.	Strong emphasis on doctrine with Christian life expected to proceed from faith in Christ. Individual and whole church to make faith active in love.
Statistics*	Membership . . . . 3,332,000 Mosques . . . . 1,200 *U. S. estimate from *The World Almanac 1999*.	

CHAPTER 18

Jehovah's Witnesses

Witnesses believe that accurate knowledge about God is essential. For this reason they print and distribute Bibles and Bible literature internationally.

Fervently zealous in their convictions, members of Jehovah's Witnesses accept the entire Bible as the Word of God and base their beliefs on it, to the exclusion of church traditions. They believe that they are the only ones who have such a view of the Bible. Since they have no clergy-laity distinctions, every one of Jehovah's Witnesses is considered a minister with the responsibility of spreading the good news of God's Kingdom.

Witnesses use the word *church* to refer to a united body of worshipers and not to a building. Ministers of the society see their chief work as bearing witness to the truth on behalf of God, whose name is Jehovah. In this way, they believe that they qualify to bear the Bible-based name, Jehovah's Witnesses.

Baptism: Symbol of Dedication

To become a minister for Jehovah, an individual is instructed to study the Bible to learn God's will, to live in harmony with it, and to make a personal dedication to God, doing so in private prayer to God. As a symbol of this dedication, a person is baptized by immersion in water. This process results in the individual's becoming an ordained minister of Jehovah God, commissioned to do his will.

Most of these ministers spend about 15 hours a month spreading the word of Jehovah, although a minority—known as Pioneers—give more than 70 hours a month. House-to-house preaching is considered a Christ-like and apostolic method. Witnesses go from door to door, using their Bibles to speak with people on themes of particular interest to the hearer. They also distribute literature containing Bible-based articles and items of current interest.

Use of Bible

Extensive use is made of the Bible by the Witnesses. Elaborately quoting from Scripture, numerous proof-texts are utilized from scattered portions of the Bible to verify their beliefs. For example, Genesis 9:4, the passage that speaks of eating meat with the blood in it, and Acts 15:28–29 are employed to prove that blood transfusions are wrong. Ecclesiastes 9:5, 10, verses that describe the unconscious state of the dead, and Acts 17:31, Paul's words regarding the hope of a future resurrection, are used to show that the dead are in the grave awaiting their resurrection to life.

A major teaching of Jehovah's Witnesses emphasizes the apocalyptic passages of the Bible dealing with the conclusion of this system of things and the restoration of Paradise on the earth.

Meeting in Halls

Witnesses gather in private homes or modest auditoriums called Kingdom Halls to study the Bible and equip themselves for preaching the Kingdom's message. The name *Kingdom Hall* puts emphasis on what Witnesses see as their main purpose: to advertise God's Kingdom as the hope of the world.

Congregations are kept small. Two are formed from one when it reaches about 200 members. The congregation schedules five meetings each week, which include instruction in the Bible, doctrine, and public speaking.

The Kingdom Hall is seen as the center of pure worship. Any Witness who willfully and unrepentantly does not live up to Bible standards, as by living an immoral life, constantly getting drunk, or habitually stealing, is subject to being *disfellowshipped.*

Instruction is also given at annual conventions. Smaller ones of 1,000 to 2,000 Witnesses in a local area are called circuit assemblies, and larger conventions of 5,000 to 20,000 or more, called district conventions, may be national or international in scope.

Origins of the Society

Witnesses claim to follow no individual person. The founder of the Watch Tower Society, Charles Taze Russell, was its first president. Russell was a layperson who gathered a group of people around him for Bible study. His guiding idea was to use the Bible as the only standard and its teachings as the only creed. Russell's group grew and by 1878 he was leader of an independent congregation. He was a prolific writer and began publishing *The Watchtower* magazine in 1879. Early in the next century the group adopted the name "Jehovah's Witnesses," from Isaiah 43:10, "You are my witnesses." Previously, they used the name Bible Students or were called by such names as Russellites or Millennial Dawnites.

Doctrinally Different

Unlike most groups that claim to follow the Christian tradition, the Witnesses do not hold to the doctrine of the Trinity. They refer to Jesus as the Son of God, not God the Son, and he is considered as subject to God, the Father, being a creation of Jehovah God. They believe that Jesus was not resurrected in a fleshly body but ascended into heaven with a spirit body after his death. Christ's life course on earth is seen as an example that Christians strive to follow.

Emphasis is placed on the coming rule of God's Kingdom over the earth, with Jesus Christ as its heavenly king. Christ is believed to have "returned" spiritually in 1914, when he began ruling in heaven as King of God's Kingdom.

Witnesses believe that through his death as a perfect man on earth, Jesus provided the ransom and opened the way for humans to be delivered from the sin and death that all have inherited because of the sin of mankind's forefather, Adam.

Witnesses believe that accurate knowledge about God is essential. For this reason, they print and distribute Bibles and Bible literature internationally. Their official journal, *The Watchtower,* has a circulation of some 22,300,000, in 130 languages.

Attitudes toward the World

Witnesses assert that the present corrupt system of things will be destroyed at God's hand during the "great tribulation," which includes the battle of Armageddon (Matthew 24:21; Revelation 7:9). Only then can Paradise be restored to earth.

Witnesses do not take part in interfaith movements. They carefully examine the doctrines of various churches and note as false any unscriptural aspects of those teachings.

Because their allegiance is to God first, Witnesses maintain strict neutrality and therefore do not bear arms in warfare or participate in the political affairs of government. They respect national flags but since they view saluting as an act of worship, they do not salute the flag of any nation. Witnesses claim to give their worship and allegiance only to God, but they affirm strict adherence to all human laws that do not conflict with God's.

Seeking to follow the pattern of the early Christians, Witnesses maintain and publish their convictions throughout the world. They claim an urgent task, for they believe Armageddon is close and the Kingdom is at hand.

For Discussion

□ Both Lutherans and Jehovah's Witnesses claim to base their beliefs on the Bible. Why, then, do you think there are such striking differences in their doctrines?
□ Because of variations from historic Christian beliefs, some question whether Jehovah's Witnesses should be considered Christian. What criteria do you think should be used to decide?
□ A centerpiece of Witness activity is proclaiming their beliefs from house to house. Do you think we should do more of that? Why or why not?

For Further Study

The following materials are all published by the Watch Tower Bible and Tract Society of Pennsylvania:
□ *The Watchtower* (magazine)
□ *Knowledge that Leads to Eternal Life* (textbook)
□ *Jehovah's Witnesses in the Twentieth Century* (tract)
□ Jehovah's Witnesses web site: www.watchtower.org

Table of Comparison	*Witnesses*	*Lutherans*
Teachings	1. Reject the Trinity. Only Jehovah worshiped as Creator and God Almighty. 2. Believe that Christ was the first creation by God. 3. Believe in a future opportunity for salvation for those who do not have such opportunity in this life. 4. Reject the idea of eternal torment for the wicked. Evil souls are annihilated.	1. Accept the triune nature of God—Father, Son, and Holy Spirit. The name "Jehovah" is a mistaken combination of Hebrew consonants and vowels. 2. Accept the divinity of Christ, the Son of God from all eternity. 3. Believe humankind's eternal destiny is determined in this life. 4. Accept the reality of judgment as taught by the Scriptures.
Type of Worship	No liturgy. Services largely Bible study and sermons. No Sunday school—children learn and worship with adults.	Liturgical pattern of worship used. Seek to nurture faith through worship and other programs.
Government	Oversight by a Governing Body. Congregations supervised by local body of elders. No clergy-laity distinctions.	Interdependent congregational, regional, national, and global expressions of the church characterized by democratic decision making, strong ecumenical relationships, elected leadership, and an ordained ministry.
Characteristics	Zealous, believing that they alone use the Bible and not human traditions as basis for belief. Baptism by immersion; communion, viewed as a memorial of Christ's death, celebrated only once a year and received by only a few called ones.	Believe that wherever Christ is confessed as Lord and Savior, Christians can be found. No emphasis on mode of Baptism; Communion offered frequently for all believers.
Statistics*	Membership ("ministers") . . . . 1,040,283 Congregations . . . . 11,064 *U. S. statistics from the Watch Tower Society.	

CHAPTER 19

Judaism

The lighting of the nine-branch candelabra on Hanukkah symbolizes God's faithfulness to the Jewish people.

As the twenty-first century begins, Judaism remains the source from which almost all Western faiths developed. That statement is ironic, however, in that Jews, not being tied to the birth of Jesus, will not be observing the twenty-first century as a new millennium. So on the one hand, Christianity marks a significant point in time, while on the other hand it still relates to Judaism as its spiritual origin. This is one small example of the significant unresolved tension in the relationship between Judaism and Christianity.

Defining Judaism adequately in this brief chapter is impossible. This means that every reader must take responsibility to find more adequate explanations than is possible here; however, it is hoped that these pages will open several doors, ask several questions, and provoke much discussion, all in the hope of creating a more dynamic relationship between Jews and Christians.

Judaism is a term that includes many facets, all of them overlapping. A full description of contemporary Jews must take into account

- a monotheistic religious identity that draws upon its roots in sacred Scripture;
- a "rabbinic" tradition of ongoing interpretation;
- a diverse history of experiences of living among other, dominant cultures;
- a complex literature of lore, law, and ritual practice;
- a modern national identity linked to a specific land and culture; and finally
- a diverse sense of ethnicity that allows for "secular" Jews.

The only statement all Jews can agree upon is this: all Jews don't believe in more than one God. Beyond that, if we define Judaism solely—or even primarily—as a religious faith then we lose sight of a significant number, maybe even a majority of those who accept the label "Jews," who do not participate in synagogue worship or home ritual. Judaism is not merely a faith among the many world religions. The terms *Jew* and *Judaism* are themselves relatively modern and cannot be applied to any scriptural description of Hebrews, Israelites, and

Judeans. We need to be clear about this, especially as we do Bible study: the Jews and Judaism of our time have *nothing* to do with any description found in the Hebrew or Christian scripture or later Church tradition.

Three Basic Concepts

The following key categories describe or define Jews and Judaism. Each requires a great deal of further development, especially in any interfaith dialogue.

God, Torah, and Israel: these three idioms are essential in any definitions of Jew and Judaism. *God* is the Creator of the universe, the Redeemer from Egyptian slavery as well as the source of Ultimate Redemption, and the Revealer of those Teachings and Law that constitute the Torah, the Word of God's Presence. The *Torah* is first the Five Books of Moses (Genesis through Deuteronomy) as "revealed" on Mt. Sinai and remains the primary source for a still expanding literature of rabbinic interpretations of ritual behavior, theology, and ethics. *Israel* describes both the actual community of people since the time of Scripture to the present and the physical geo-political-cultural reality of the Land of Israel throughout history. These three ideas or ideals remain in a state of constant tension from the time of Scripture to the present.

Through the centuries, through the many different cultures, Jewish interpretations of God have gone through many adaptations. Humankind is the purposeful creation of God. From the time of Abraham in scripture through the present, Jews understand themselves to be in a covenant relationship with God. In this covenant, both personal and transcendent, the opportunity to engage in the observance of *Mitzvot*—Commandments—links Jews as individuals within a community to God.

Scripture provides the initial 613 *Mitzvot* (Christians generally think of only 10!) that are continually interpreted by rabbinic authority in every age. Thus, while Scripture provides the initial commandment, it is the rabbinic interpretation, from the third century until the present, that defines the specific behavior, such as Sabbath observance, wedding ceremonies, ethical guides, and liturgical services.

Of all the essential foundational ideas/ideals, Israel is the most complex to explain. We are a community with varied ethnic and cultural differences: *Ashkenazi* Jews come from Central and Eastern Europe and make up the vast majority of Jews most readers will engage; *Sephardi* Jews are Western European, Spanish, North African and native-born Israelis. Each of these major categories has many separate specific dialects, ritual, and liturgical identities. Israel is also the complex reality of a modern nation-state since 1948, and has its own independent language, culture, history, and religious/political factors.

It is important to understand that not all Israelis are Jews and not all Jews are connected to the State of Israel. It also goes without saying that the "Israelites" in Scripture have nothing to do with today's Israelis. Nor do the "Jews" depicted, say, in *Fiddler on the Roof* or *Schindler's List* have anything to do with either the Hebrews or "Jews" described in most Hebrew/Christian Scripture (Old/New Testaments). One must be very careful to determine what the term *Jew* means in each instance.

Holy Time

Judaism has a rich weekly and annual calendar. The holiest day in the Jewish calendar is *Shabbat*, the Sabbath, which begins on Friday night at sundown and concludes on Saturday at sundown. The Sabbath is linked to both the creation of the universe and the Exodus from Egypt. Jews traditionally initiate the

Sabbath as well as other holy days by lighting at least two candles, saying a blessing over wine or grape juice and a blessing over the bread ("challah" in Hebrew). This Sabbath home meal is understood to be a very significant family/communal religious experience. Synagogue services are Friday evening and Saturday morning.

The fall cycle of holy days begins with *Rosh HaShannah* (New Year), continues with the Ten Days of Repentance, and then concludes with *Yom Kippur* (Day of Atonement). These are called the High Holy Days. *Sukkot* (the Feast of Tabernacles) goes for seven to eight days and concludes with *Simhat Torah* (Rejoicing with the Torah). *Hanukkah,* The Feast of Lights, commemorates a military victory by the Judeans over the Assyrian Greeks in the year 165 B.C.E. Legend has it that when the temple was rededicated there was not enough consecrated oil to light the candelabra or *Menorah,* but that the small amount miraculously lasted eight days. This is reenacted every year by the lighting of a nine-branch candelabra, *Hannukiah*. This festival is *not* comparable in any religious value to Christmas, though both share a common winter solstice timing. *Purim,* a festival based on the book of Esther, is usually midwinter and commemorates a Persian folk tale and national threat to Jewish survival.

Pesach, or Passover, is probably the most observed home festival with the Seder meal and retelling of the story of the Exodus in the *Haggadah*. During the seven to eight days of the festival, Jews do not eat any leavening but rather *Matzah* and other special Passover food. Unlike *Hanukkah,* which has no religious parallel to Christmas, Passover is fundamentally linked to Easter. The Last Supper was by tradition a Seder meal shared by Jesus and his disciples, all of whom were Jews. It has become relatively common for churches to have a "mock" Seder in order to connect with this Jewish ritual act from which so much Christian ritual later comes. *Shavuot,* Pentecost, is the late spring/early summer festival that completes the cycle of pilgrimage festivals noted in Scripture: *Sukkot, Pesach, Shavuot*. Today most non-Orthodox contemporary Jews observe Shavuot as a significant public completion of Jewish education (tenth grade) linked to the tradition that this was the festival that remembers the giving of the Torah at Mt. Sinai.

All of these holy days have specific rituals, liturgies, and distinctive symbols that further reading will provide. Like most contemporary Christians, Jews attend services most intensely during the four services of the High Holy Days (much like Christmas and Easter) and some Sabbath eve/morning services. Two significant observances which link Jews to their modern history are *Yom HaShoah* (the Holocaust Memorial Day) and *Yom HaAtzmaut* (Israeli Independence Day). Both of these underscore the importance of the ethnic link that most Jews have with their contemporary sense of destiny.

Jewish History

Scripture begins with creation and thus we trace our history in the "universal" (before the chosen people were identified) first 11 chapters of Genesis. Judaism's particular history begins with Genesis 12 and Abraham and continues through the scriptural narratives, Prophets, and finally the Writings (Psalms, Proverbs, Job, and so forth). Thus, the first element of Jewish history is biblical and concludes with 168 B.C.E. (before the common era), in the time of the Greek domination and Hanukkah.

From 168 B.C.E. to 1000 C.E. is the Rabbinic period, during which the great interpretative texts of Jewish law and lore were developed, written, and edited. This is the first great period of *Diaspora Jewry,* the dispersion of Jews throughout the world after the destruction of the temple in 70 C.E. by Rome. The texts reflect Jewish life adapting to non-Jewish cultures and the development of rabbis—teachers—in place of a priesthood and sacrifices in the temple. The *Mishnah* (assembled around 200 C.E.) and then the *Gemara* (500 C.E.) together make up the great body of Jewish law called the *Talmud* that continues to influence how Judaism is practiced. Later legal texts were interpretations and commentaries of these primary texts. During this period several *Midrashim*—sermonic interpretations—were also produced, several of which represent the mystical strain of Judaism.

The medieval period 1000–1650 C.E. is primarily a history of Jewish relations with the dominant cultures and religions of Christianity and Islam. The literature becomes more philosophical, featuring such luminaries as Maimonides and HaLevi. During this period a great deal of painful material represents a tormented relationship between Judaism and Christianity. Any careful examination of Jews and Judaism must stop and try to understand the centuries of contempt between our two faith identities. Jews were expelled from every Christian country in Europe except for Holland and the Scandinavian countries. This history of mistrust and persecution is the foundation for many of the issues we are still trying to understand and forgive today.

Finally, the modern period, from 1650 C.E. to the present, is about Jews moving throughout Europe and eventually North America and their creative adaptation to the Enlightenment. The movements of Judaism—Reform, Orthodox, Conservative, and Reconstructionism—are all products of this period of immigration and acculturation. One can trace liberal and rational movements, then a reaction emphasizing tradition, another reaction of a midpoint between liberal and traditional as experienced in America, and finally a very contemporary attempt of naturalism and community traditions as still another attempt to bridge the liberal and the traditional. These movements each have their own ideologies, liturgies, communal authorities, seminaries, and publications but are not "sects," and all share the basics of Judaism as described above. Most large cities have Temples (Reform), Synagogues (Conservative), and Shuls (Orthodox) to which guests are welcome, and many rabbis are willing to engage in dialogue with Christian churches.

The two most extraordinary events of contemporary Jewish history are the Holocaust and the establishment of the State of Israel. The destruction of six million Jews in Europe is fundamental to any sense of identity for a Jew today. Jews do not deny that another 5.2 million non-Jews were also killed, but the Holocaust is a unique act of genocide that should not be trivialized by comparing it to other horrible acts of mass destruction. To be Jew today ultimately means making a conscious "choice" in the face of Hitler's plan to exterminate *all* Jews.

The physical reality of Israel as a Jewish homeland has also had a transforming impact on Jewish identity. For the first time since the destruction of the temple and the beginning of the Diaspora, Jews can chose to live in a country ruled by and for a Jewish majority. The difference between the religious and cultural Jewish identity in Israel and in the rest of the world Jewish community is immense and is a source of great inner struggle for the Jewish community. The current political power of ultra-Orthodox Jews in the Israeli Parliament has created a dangerous division among world Jewry, and confuses non-Jewish Americans for whom these kind of "religious wars" ended long ago. No understanding of contemporary Jews and Judaism is possible without a careful consideration of what it means for Jews to live after Auschwitz and with a vibrant Jewish state.

Life Cycles

Like all faith communities, Jews have specific ritual acts marking occasions from birth through death, but none of these are either sacraments or sacramental, merely family and personal occasions for private and communal celebrations. There are significant differences among the movements of Judaism, especially as it relates to the equality of gender and most recently sexual orientation. These differences simply reflect the attempts by Jews and Judaism to adapt to the challenges of the twenty-first century.

□ *Bris,* baby naming: On the eighth day after birth, a male child is circumcised by a *mohel* (a person qualified to circumcise) and given a Hebrew name. The origin of the ceremony is Genesis 15. Many communities now name baby girls on the eighth day in a ceremony of covenant.

□ *Bar/Bat(Bas) Mitzvah* is a public ceremony that celebrates when a boy or girl reaches the age of 13 and is considered for ritual purposes an adult in the Jewish community. The ceremony, which takes place most commonly in a temple/synagogue on Sabbath morning, has the teen leading the worship service and reading from the Torah scroll and then teaching what they have learned. The ceremony culminates several years of learning Hebrew and scripture; its origin is not located in Scripture or rabbinic literature. Many Reform, Conservative, and Reconstructionist congregations have a ceremony called "Confirmation" that was originally borrowed from Lutheran churches in Germany. Confirmation today marks later teen completion of a phase of religious education.

□ The Jewish wedding ceremony is a public act in which the two people exchange vows under a *chupah,* wedding canopy, after signing a *ketubah,* wedding contract in front of two witnesses. According to Jewish law no rabbi is required, though by modern convention the rabbi acts on behalf of the civil authority. The particularity of a Jewish wedding is highlighted in the final idiom of the vows, *"... k'dat moshe v'israel,"* "according to the law of Moses and Israel." This vow does not allow for the anomaly of an interfaith wedding service. This rabbi feels strongly that any attempt to create a hybrid ritual blending Judaism and Christianity is inappropriate and should not be considered when a Jew and Christian choose to marry. Such couples should accept the differences which define their faith communities and have a civil ceremony. This choice honestly affirms the truths of both Judaism and Christianity.

□ The rituals for mourning among Jews are very extensive. Basic elements include a funeral during which the Psalms and modern readings are recited and a eulogy given, followed by a burial in the ground, usually in a wooden coffin in a consecrated Jewish cemetery. For seven days following the funeral the family "sits *Shiva*" at home and accepts visits and has services in the evening. Many non-Orthodox observe this for three days. At the end of one year (eleven months) there is a dedication of the head stone/grave marker. On the anniversary of the death—*Yahrzeit*—the name of the deceased is read during services and the mourners rise to say *Kaddish,* the mourners prayer.

The aim of this chapter has been to whet your appetite for further exploration into Judaism. The resources listed below could help provide information. The best way to understand Jews and Judaism is to engage in dialogue, so having your minister or teacher contact a rabbi and creating an exchange will provide a wonderful way to learn more.

For Discussion

□ In what ways can you tell that Christianity developed out of the Jewish faith?
□ Talk about how this article has helped you to distinguish between the Jews or Israelites of the Bible and modern Jews.
□ Think of ways in which our society assumes that people are Christian. How can avoiding this assumption make our lives richer?

For Further Study

□ *What Is a Jew* by Rabbi Morris Kertzer (Cleveland: World Publishing, 1960)
□ *Living Judaism* by Rabbi Wayne Dosick (Harper San Francisco, 1995)
□ *A History of the Jews* by Paul Johnson (New York: Harper & Row, 1987)
□ Reform Judaism web site: www.rj.org Conservative: www.uscj.org unofficial Orthodox web site: www.us-israel.org

Table of Comparison	*Judaism*	*Lutherans*
Teachings	1. Everlasting covenant between God and Israel is rooted in God's love. The Torah reveals God's will for the people and is obeyed by the people in faith as their part in the covenant. 2. The Torah is the complete guide for Jewish life. In its more narrow sense, it may refer to all Jewish writings, the Hebrew Bible (Old Testament), or the Pentateuch (first five books of the Bible). 3. Human beings created good and in the likeness of God. Able to fulfill God's will by living according to the Torah. Sin is a human action that violates God's will.	1. Since humanity rebelled against God, God sent Jesus into the world to establish a new covenant so that all people might believe and be saved. 2. Accept the Bible (Old and New Testament) as the written witness of God's revelation of saving action through Jesus Christ. Jesus Christ is the key to interpreting the Bible. 3. Human beings created good and in the likeness of God but are by nature sinful as a consequence of the fall. Sin is a condition that can only be overcome through Jesus Christ.
Type of Worship	Worship is centered in the home and synagogue. The synagogue is a place of prayer, learning, and social activity.	Worship is centered in the church. The church defines itself as the community where the gospel is proclaimed and the sacraments administered.
Government	Reform congregations are autonomous; Conservative and Orthodox congregations are subject to the rules and principles applied within their movements. Each congregation is led by ordained rabbi(s) and an elected board of laypeople.	Interdependent congregational, regional, national, and global expressions of the church characterized by democratic decision making, strong ecumenical relationships, elected leadership, and an ordained ministry.
Characteristics	Emphasis on being Jewish as a way of life. Tremendous cultural and historical differences of background that can be traced to its long history of being a scattered people. Well organized in many national Jewish organizations that promote education and human rights.	Emphasis on doctrine, with Christian practice supposed to proceed from faith in Christ. Historically a denomination of northern Europeans with common ethnic and cultural background. Ecumenically aware, but historically cautious about entering into the political arena.
Statistics*	Synagogue Membership......... 3,500,000 Congregations .... 2,440 *U. S. statistics of three bodies—Reform, Conservative, and Orthodox—from *The World Almanac 1999*.	

CHAPTER 20

Latter-day Saints

Following the murder of their prophet Joseph Smith in 1844, the Latter-day Saints traveled west from Illinois to what is now Utah.

The Church of Jesus Christ of Latter-day Saints, sometimes referred to by the unofficial name Mormon Church, is a worldwide church with a total membership exceeding 10 million. At the present rate of growth, the membership will reach approximately 20 million by the year 2010.

This church, organized at Fayette, New York, on April 6, 1830, is not an offshoot of any existing church of the time, but claims to be a restoration of the Church of Jesus Christ, established by Jesus of Nazareth when he lived upon the earth.

Continuing Revelations

The Latter-day Saints believe that both the Old and New Testaments contain the Word of God, and profess to have the same church organization that existed in the primitive church.

They believe that revelations were given and will continue to be given to all people who seek God. Joseph Smith, founder of this church, published *The Book of Mormon* in 1830 that is said to contain a translation of ancient records. The *Doctrine and Covenants* (1835) contains revelations given to Joseph Smith, with some additions given by his successors. Another book, *The Pearl of Great Price* (1851) is a selection of materials from the revelations, translations, and narrations of Joseph Smith, including the Articles of Faith, a brief statement of principal doctrines of the church. Because of the nature of its origin and claim to divine authority, the church does not join any ecumenical movement.

Seeking a New Zion

This church, after its organization in New York state, was persecuted by its neighbors, causing a move to Ohio in 1831. Desiring to set up a new Zion, most of the membership moved westward from Ohio to Missouri during the years 1831–38. Conflict over the slavery issue (the members were largely from New England), cooperative buying and selling, and sharp differences in religious beliefs resulted in mob uprisings that resulted in the "Saints," as they were called, being driven from the state of Missouri, a slave state. The fleeing church members were welcomed into Illinois, where between 1839 and 1846 they built the prosperous city of Nauvoo, for a time the largest city in that state.

Following the murder of their prophet, Joseph Smith, and his brother Hyrum by a mob in 1844, the church's membership again turned their faces westward. The winter of 1846–47 was spent by some 16,000 members upon the western plains. In 1847 the advance companies of the exiles traveled some 1,100 miles across plain and desert and settled in the Great Basin centering at what is now Salt Lake City.

During the course of the next 30 years, under the leadership of Brigham Young, 375 colonies were established in the western Rocky Mountain area—the beginnings of many of the cities now existing there. The first civil government was known as the Provisional State of Deseret (1849–51). Utah was organized as a United States territory in 1850 and continued as a territory until 1896 when statehood was achieved.

Emphasis on Education

The Saints organized schools wherever they went. What is now the University of Utah was first established by the church as the University of Deseret in 1850. Latter-day Saint educators are to be found in nearly every major higher learning institution in the United States.

Committed to a philosophy that real education necessitates instruction in both secular and religious subjects, the Latter-day Saints have seminaries adjacent to public high schools and Institutes of Religion adjacent to colleges and universities where students may supplement secular education with religious instruction.

God and Humankind

The Latter-day Saints believe that people are created in the image of God, and that God is a being of body, parts, and passions, a supreme being separate and apart from the bodily form of Jesus Christ who is literally the Son of God.

They accept the biblical account of Jesus Christ as found in the gospels, the letters, and other writings of the New Testament. These are seen as representing Jesus as the literal Son of God in the flesh, as having taught the perfect gospel, as being in frequent communication with his Father during his ministry, of performing mighty miracles, of dying upon the cross to save humankind, and of rising from the dead with his actual body of flesh and bones which he showed to many disciples.

They believe that the Holy Ghost, or Spirit, is a being without body, through whom the Father and the Son may communicate with humankind and achieve the work of the Godhead.

The Latter-day Saints claim that additional teachings of the Christ were found in America on ancient gold plates and translated into English by Joseph Smith. This account is published as *The Book of Mormon* and has a circulation exceeding 90 million copies.

This church believes that humankind is eternal, that people are the literal offspring of God; and that people existed in a spiritual body before earth-life, and will live again in the spirit world and eventually be resurrected with a body of flesh and bone. Humankind may progress eternally and may become as the gods. Marriage, when performed by the priesthood in sacred temples of the church, continues beyond this life.

Church Organization

The Church of Jesus Christ of Latter-day Saints is founded upon authority claimed to have been received directly from the resurrected Christ through divine messengers: John the Baptist, Peter, James, and John, as well as the ancient prophets Moses, Elias, and Elijah. Through this priesthood authority the church was organized, and by such priesthood authority the church is governed.

The priesthood is held in varying degrees by most of the male members of the church 12 years of age and older, who constitute a vast body of volunteer workers. Women have equal sustaining vote in the church and find places as teachers and officers in Relief Society, Sunday school, Primary, and the Young Women's auxiliary.

A prophet is at the head of this church with counselors, a quorum of Twelve Apostles, The Quorums of the Seventy, and a Presiding Bishopric. These constitute what is known as the General Authorities.

The church is divided into ecclesiastical and geographical divisions called *stakes*, each presided over by three high priests and a high council of twelve. They are also unpaid lay members. Each stake is divided geographically into wards, usually five or more. Each ward is presided over by a bishop and two counselors to the bishop, with one or more ward clerks. All are lay members and receive no salary.

Baptism and Meeting

Membership is gained in this church through Baptism by immersion by one holding priesthood authority. Infants are not baptized. Children are baptized when they reach the age of accountability, defined as the age of eight. Following Baptism, the Holy Ghost is conferred by the laying on of hands by those holding the Melchizedek Priesthood.

The principal worship service, a *sacrament meeting*, is held each Sunday where the emblems of the sacrament, bread and water, are blessed by priests or elders of the church and administered to the members.

Missionary Work

This church is concerned with every aspect of life and carries on an elaborate program to foster health, recreation, care of the poor, education, the arts, and the general welfare of its members. It maintains strict separation of church and state, but urges full participation of its members in the civic and political processes of their respective nations.

Some 330 missions covering most of the globe are maintained. About 60,000 missionaries are kept in these missions, serving at their own expense for an average of 24 months. Other missionaries serve on a part-time basis in the various stakes of The Church of Jesus Christ of Latter-day Saints. The missionary zeal accounts for much of the growth of church membership.

For Discussion

□ In many instances, beliefs of Latter-day Saints are similar to historic Christian teachings, but with some variation. Can you find examples of this?

□ How do you think the American beginnings of the Church of Latter-day Saints have helped, and hindered, its growth?

□ An interesting historical comparison can be made between The Church of Jesus Christ of Latter-day Saints and Islam. What similarities and differences can you see in their development?

For Further Study

- *The Encyclopedia of Mormonism* (Macmillan Publishing, 1991), 4 vols., available in many libraries.
- *A Latter-day Saint Library* (Infobases, 1998) Multi-work CD-ROM.
- *Mormon Standard Time* by Clayton C. Newell (St. Martin's Press, 2000)
- Latter-day Saints Web site: www.lds.org

Table of Comparison	*Latter-day Saints*	*Lutherans*
Teachings	1. Believe in God, the Eternal Father, in Jesus Christ, God's Son, and in the Holy Ghost; these three considered separate personages but one in purpose.	1. Confess the unity of the triune God: Father, Son, and Holy Spirit.
	2. Believe the Bible to be the Word of God. Also believe *The Book of Mormon.* Accept revelations received by the prophets of the present Latter-day Saints.	2. Believe the Bible is the written witness to God's revelation of saving purpose through Jesus Christ. Christ is the great revelation of God; contrary revelations to Christ are rejected.
	3. Believe revelation has not ceased; new ones may come at any time.	3. Believe the New Testament faith was "once for all delivered."
	4. Reject original sin. Children are considered born innocent and cannot sin until they understand right from wrong.	4. Believe all people are born under bondage to evil; power of God's grace needed to free humankind from this captivity.
	5. Reject infant baptism since children are believed to be without sin. Baptism for the dead. Immersion only, by one holding authority.	5. Baptize infants. Do not reject any method of baptism. Baptism for dead seen as contrary to Scripture.
	6. Communion considered a symbol, a renewing of covenants with Christ. The emblems of bread and water used.	6. Affirm the real presence of Christ in the sacrament of Communion. Elements of bread and wine used.
Type of Worship	No liturgy. Communion celebrated every Sunday. No formally trained or paid ministry to lead the service.	Liturgical pattern of worship used with Communion celebrated regularly. Ordained ministry.
Characteristics	Consider both Bible and *The Book of Mormon* as authorities. Rapid growth.	Consider Bible as only authority for faith and life, with God's grace through Word and sacrament.
Statistics*	Membership . . . . 4,800,000 Congregations . . . . 11,000 *U.S. statistics from *Yearbook of American and Canadian Churches 1998.*	

CHAPTER 21

The Lutheran Church—Missouri Synod

Martin Luther's translation of scripture into the language of the people (German) lays a foundation for the LCMS view that the Bible teaches the one way of salvation in Jesus Christ.

The Lutheran Church—Missouri Synod (LCMS) has always taken its confession of faith seriously. Such confessional seriousness prompted a determined group to leave its homeland in Germany when it became convinced that the unhindered expression of Lutheran teaching was no longer possible in its native Saxony, where rationalism prevailed. Risking everything, approximately 750 Lutherans crossed the Atlantic in 1838 under the direction of Martin Stephan. Four of five ships arrived safely in New Orleans. The fledgling group came up the Mississippi River and settled in Perry County, Missouri (south of St. Louis), a year later.

Trauma soon followed. Stephan, their esteemed leader, was charged with sexual immorality and was expelled from the community. The leadership vacuum was filled by young C. F. W. Walther (1811–1887), who emerged as the theological spokesperson for a disillusioned group struggling to regain its spiritual and doctrinal bearings in an entirely foreign cultural setting. Finally, after a time of intense study and debate, and then after years of communication with other North American Lutherans of similar confessional persuasion, the German Evangelical Lutheran Synod of Missouri, Ohio, and Other States was born in 1847, numbering 12 congregations and about 3,500 souls. Walther would be its preeminent teacher and pastor, whether officially or otherwise, for four decades. The adjective "German" remained until World War I, as Missouri retained its ethnic identity longer than most American Lutheran groups. The name was finally shortened to *The Lutheran Church—Missouri Synod* in 1947.

Doctrine and Life

The Missouri Synod has been characterized by a polity of congregational interdependence, a commitment to Christian education at all levels (and especially at the elementary school level—its school system being perhaps its best-known feature among those otherwise unfamiliar with Missouri's doctrine and practice), diligent pastoral care, invitations to pursue unity with other like-minded American

Lutherans, innovative and varied evangelism efforts, and extensive overseas missions. These activities were consistently built upon an uncompromising affirmation of biblical authority and truthfulness, and by a conscientious commitment to the sixteenth-century Lutheran Confessions. (These Confessions include the Apostles', Nicene, and Athanasian creeds, the Augsburg Confession and its Apology, Luther's Small and Large Catechisms, the Smalcald Articles and the Treatise on the Power and Primacy of the Pope, and the Formula of Concord.)

The Synod's efforts have been blessed with numerical growth, most dramatically during the latter part of the nineteenth century and the first half of the twentieth century. Today the LCMS has about 2.6 million members in approximately 6,200 congregations. Its educational system numbers nearly 1,800 elementary schools, more than 60 high schools, a 10-school university system, and two seminaries. Geographically, the Missouri Synod is strongest in the Midwestern United States.

The doctrine and practice of the Missouri Synod intentionally reflects the priorities of Holy Scripture and the Lutheran Confessions. At the center of Scripture and at the core of the confessional writings is God's justification of the ungodly by grace, for the sake of Jesus Christ, through faith—all without any human preparation or cooperation.

From the days of Walther to the present—and again following the emphases of Martin Luther, Philip Melanchthon, and the other confessional authors—the Missouri Synod has emphasized law and gospel as the two principal teachings into which Scripture is divided. The law exposes human sinfulness, while the gospel is God's definitive and final promise of forgiveness, life, and salvation to those who are broken and helpless in the face of the law's indictment. The message of salvation is communicated to sinners through the spoken Word of absolution and through the sacraments of Baptism and the Lord's Supper, and it is such Word and sacrament that gives the basic structure to the Lutheran liturgy. Through these means of grace alone the triune God creates and sustains the church, which in turn can be recognized by the presence of this same quickening Word and these two sacraments. The Missouri Synod sees the "body of doctrine" as an organic whole that is unified and informed by the gospel, and it views the entire Bible, both the Old and New Testaments, as teaching one way of salvation in Jesus Christ.

Shaped by Controversy

The history of the Missouri Synod has not been without controversy. In its earliest years, Walther helped the infant community work through issues pertaining to the doctrines of church and ministry. On the basis of Scripture, the Lutheran Confessions, and especially the writings of Martin Luther, Walther was able both to reassure the Saxons of their churchly identity and to preserve the balance between the divine institution of the pastoral office and the rights and privileges of the priesthood of all believers. Near the turn of the twentieth century Walther, and then his successor, Francis Pieper, wrote extensively on the doctrine of God's eternal election, stressing not only that salvation is from beginning to end God's accomplishment in Jesus Christ, but also that God had chosen his children in Christ from eternity.

Just as the controversy over election helps explain alliances among American Lutheran groups at the turn of the twentieth century, so the configuration of American Lutheranism today is in part a consequence of the most serious controversy the Missouri Synod faced during the 1960s and 1970s. From Missouri's perspective (and vastly oversimplified), this debate focused on the authority and interpretation of the Bible. "Biblical criticism" (in which the biblical text is analyzed using sophisticated scholarly methods applicable to any other literature) had become fairly common in several other American Lutheran church bodies, and by the 1960s it was appearing in Missouri Synod classrooms and pulpits. For some in the synod, biblical criticism compromised the truthfulness of Scripture and potentially undermined the historical foundations of the gospel itself. Others argued that this was a misunderstanding. They regarded the so-called historical critical method as a neutral tool that could, if used properly, aid in biblical interpretation. A complicated sequence of events reached its climax in 1973 and 1974: the doctrinal position of the majority of the Concordia Seminary (St. Louis) faculty was condemned, Concordia's president was suspended, the same faculty and most students declined to continue their work under a new administration, and eventually the faculty majority and president were dismissed. The events at Concordia Seminary had their counterparts in other areas and agencies of the Synod. Sadly, all efforts at conciliation failed. Approximately 225 congregations and roughly four percent of total synodical membership left Missouri to form the Association of Evangelical Lutheran Churches in 1976, which would become part of the Evangelical Lutheran Church of America in 1988. (The LCMS itself has never been part of a major merger.)

How Much Agreement?

These more recent controversies color the landscape of American Lutheran relations down to the present day. The initial debates of the 1960s and 1970s have given rise to another cluster of issues, and most particularly to the question of how much agreement is necessary before Christians can worship and celebrate the sacraments together. The Missouri Synod sees its confession of faith as requiring agreement in "the gospel in all its articles" (following the principle of one the confessional writings noted earlier, the Formula of Concord). In the eyes of many Missourians, their sisters and brothers in the ELCA seem to maintain that a more basic agreement in the gospel and a less comprehensive doctrinal confession is sufficient. Indeed, as a past president of the Missouri Synod has winsomely observed, Missouri and the ELCA disagree about the significance of disagreeing!

Missouri continues to address issues of confessional identity as its enters the twenty-first century. Internal conflict did not end with the difficulties of the 1970s. Perhaps the most challenging issue facing Missourians today is the basic question of what it means to be a confessional Lutheran church body in an age when American Christians seem increasingly less denominationally conscious or concerned.

At its best, the LCMS seeks to keep the gospel central in its total congregational life, in its mission work across the globe, in its educational institutions, and even in its deliberative assemblies. It aspires to be faithful and attentive to Holy Scripture, from which alone it hears God's announcement of forgiveness in Jesus Christ. Finally, it strives to echo the evangelical confession of faith made by its sixteenth-century forebears in the *Book of Concord*. Its history is not an unbroken success story; nevertheless, it is the story of a people for whom God has kept his saving promises and whom God has blessed in a measure beyond anything a struggling group of immigrants could ever have imagined.

For Discussion

□ From what you know, where would you stand on the question of how to interpret the Bible?

□ How much agreement do you think should be necessary before people can worship together? Before they can take Communion together?

For Further Study

□ *Moving Frontiers,* ed. Carl S. Meyer (St. Louis: Concordia Publishing House, 1964)

□ *Heritage in Motion,* ed. August Svelflow (St. Louis: Concordia Publishing House, 1998)

□ The Lutheran Church—Missouri Synod Web site: www.lcms.org

Table of Comparison	*Missouri Synod*	*ELCA*
Teachings	1. Believe in the triune God—Father, Son, and Holy Spirit. 2. Accept the Lutheran Confessions as true teachings of biblical faith. 3. Believe that God comes to us through the Word and the sacraments of Baptism and Holy Communion. 4. Teach justification by grace through faith. 5. Believe that the Bible should not be subjected to higher critical methods. 6. Believe that the Bible restricts women from certain church positions including ordained ministry. 7. High degree of doctrinal agreement necessary before fellowship is possible.	1. Same. 2. Same. 3. Same. 4. Same. 5. Believe that the Bible can speak effectively through use of higher critical study. 6. Believe that the Bible permits, even encourages, full participation by women in life of church. 7. Agreement on a more basic level is sufficient for fellowship.
Type of Worship	Mostly liturgical, following classical form of Western church.	Same.
Government	Congregational form with some supervision at district and national levels.	Interdependent congregational, synodical, regional, and national "expressions."
Characteristics	Strong stand on authority of the Bible, generally hesitant to enter into ecumenical alliances.	Teachings based on gospel as found in Bible. Open to alliances that promote the gospel.
Statistics*	Membership . . . . 2,601,144 Congregations . . . . 6,099 *U.S. statistics from *Yearbook of American and Canadian Churches 1998.*	

CHAPTER 22

Mennonite Church

The Amish, one branch of Mennonites, meet for worship in homes rather than church buildings.

On any Sunday you will find Mennonites gathered for worship in about 61 countries around the world. They now number more than one million, and more than half live in Africa, Asia, and South America. Mennonites are multicultural, with a wide variety of practices and people: from a "plain" Pennsylvania farmer to a California university professor; from an African American businesswoman to a Hispanic physician; from an African chieftain to a South American sociologist. The Mennonite Church in the U.S., one of several branches, currently numbers more than 355,000 members in 3,000 congregations.

Mennonites trace their beginnings to the sixteenth century Protestant Reformation in Europe. A small group of believers were convinced that Martin Luther and Ulrich Zwingli had not gone far enough in their reforms. Conrad Grebel, son of an important Swiss family, led this group in an attempt to recover New Testament Christianity. They baptized one another at Zurich, Switzerland, in January 1525, thus sparking a more "radical reformation," called the Anabaptist movement.

These believers were called Anabaptists by their opponents because in rejecting infant baptism, they re- (*ana* in Greek) baptized adults. By rejecting infant baptism they defied the state-church authorities and found themselves to be considered heretics. They were hunted down and killed as enemies of God and the state. Thousands died as martyrs by burning, beheading, or drowning. Accounts of their suffering and death were recorded in the *Martyrs Mirror,* stories that continue to be told and retold.

Though Anabaptists were hunted and killed, most refused to use the sword, even in self-defense. They read the Bible through the lens of the Sermon on the Mount, and thus followed Jesus' call to practice nonviolent love and mutual aid.

Persecution scattered the Anabaptists throughout Europe. Because of their zealous evangelism the movement spread rapidly. In the Netherlands a Catholic priest named Menno Simons (from whose name comes the title *Mennonites*) joined the movement in 1536. He became an evangelist and shepherd of the scattered Anabaptists in the Netherlands and north Germany. Though a reward of 100 Guilders was offered for his capture, Menno avoided arrest and served the movement for 25 years.

While toleration came first to Mennonites in the Netherlands, where some became wealthy, persecution continued in other parts of Western Europe. Mennonites emigrated to North America beginning in 1681.

Amish and Hutterites

The Amish and the Hutterites are a part of the original Anabaptist movement. The Hutterites trace their origin to Jacob Hutter, who died a martyr in Austria in 1536. With him they lay emphasis on the importance of sharing material possessions as a sign of love and grace. Many self-sufficient colonies have been established by them in Canada and the northern states. The Hutterites use all available modern machinery but also stress nonconformity to culture in dress and attitude, using such texts as 1 John 2:15a, "Do not love the world or the things in the world."

The Amish arose because of a problem all Christians face in trying to follow Christ in a sinful world. In 1693 Jacob Amman broke with the Swiss Mennonites when he called for stronger church discipline and greater separation from the world. To this day the Amish refuse to conform to their surrounding culture, dressing in seventeenth century garb, refusing to use cars or other modern machinery, and meeting in homes rather than church buildings for worship.

Emphasis on the Bible

Mennonites believe in the inspiration of the entire Bible, looking to the Old Testament for God's way with his people of old and to the New Testament as a guide for faith and life today. They have no objection to the Apostles' Creed and use it occasionally in their worship services. All persons being baptized first give an oral statement of faith to the congregation.

The Bible is also the guide to the kind of congregations Mennonites seek to build. They believe that every member has been given gifts by the Holy Spirit to use for the common good (1 Corinthians 12). Consequently, the central task of the pastor is to help equip every member to minister to his or her greatest potential.

Mennonites believe that Christian living means participating in Christ's work in the world. This means a readiness to suffer. It means taking Jesus' words seriously as they are recorded in the Sermon on the Mount (Matthew 5–7); believing that it is possible to obey Jesus' commandments today.

Mennonites have no sacraments which confer invisible grace. The ordinances of baptism and the Lord's supper are symbols recalling the finished work of Christ, preparing the believer for a life of obedience and discipleship.

With other Christians, Mennonites believe that human beings are sinners in need of redemption. But sin is not something people are born with, it is a problem of the will. This means that children are innocent of sin until they have reached the age of knowing right from wrong and its long-range implications. Then the children are accountable for their sins.

Service throughout the World

North American Mennonites began organizing home and foreign missions in the late 1800s. They sent a first wave of missionaries overseas during the years 1899–1915, and another round of mission expansion followed World War II.

To coordinate their relief and service programs, Mennonites organized the Mennonite Central Committee (MCC) in 1920. The Mennonite World Conference was founded in 1925 for fellowship with the global church.

With love as the primary motive, Mennonites seek to serve others at their point of need—race, peace, or poverty—knowing all the while that God is the Lord of history and that they are called to be God's helpers in the world. God's rule will be perfect on earth only when Christ returns.

For Discussion

□ Many Mennonites make visible their separateness from the world. What do you think of that as a strategy for the Christian life?

□ What differences do you find in the Mennonite understanding of baptism compared to that of your church?

For Further Study

□ *An Introduction to Mennonite History* by Cornelius J. Dyck (Scottsdale, Penn: Herald Press, 1993)

□ *Building on the Rock* by Walfred J. Fahrer (Scottdale: Herald Press, 1995)

□ Mennonite Web site: www.mennonites.org

Table of Comparison	*Mennonites*	*Lutherans*
Teachings	1. The Bible is guide for faith and life. 2. Two ordinances considered to be signs and symbols. 3. Voluntary church membership, no infant baptism. 4. Faith means obedience to Christ. 5. Believe in triune nature of God. 6. Nonviolent peacemaking is advocated.	1. The Bible is the written witness to God's revelation of saving action through Jesus Christ. 2. Two sacraments—Baptism and Communion—celebrated as means of grace. 3. Infants and adults received into the church by Baptism. 4. Justification by grace through faith. 5. Same. 6. Though peacemaking is valued, no defined position on peace and war.
Type of Worship	Nonliturgical with sermon central; often shared preaching and prayers. Singing sometimes unaccompanied. Simple, functional architecture.	Liturgical with both Word and sacrament emphasized. Rich musical heritage reflected and continued. Church architecture used to symbolize relationship with God.
Government	Congregations are autonomous, but participate in the Mennonite World Conference and other Mennonite conferences for fellowship.	Interdependent congregational, regional, national, and global expressions of the church characterized by democratic decision making, strong ecumenical relationships, elected leadership, and an ordained ministry.
Characteristics	Emphasize obedience to Christ; mission, peace, and service conscious.	Emphasize correct doctrine with faith to be lived in love; mission and service conscious.
Statistics*	Membership . . . . 355,221 Congregations . . . . 3,208 *U. S. statistics from *Yearbook of American and Canadian Churches 1998*.	

CHAPTER 23

Methodist Church

The Methodist movement in America spread quickly by the preaching of circuit riders.

The United Methodist Church is a worldwide denomination that traces its roots back to England and before, yet it has adapted well to the American culture. It grew in this country through the efforts of "circuit riders," and today it continues to preach God's love among the many cultures that make up our society.

Methodist Beginnings

The Methodist movement started in England under the leadership of John Wesley, a clergyman of the Church of England, in the eighteenth century. Wesley went outside the Church of England and organized small societies of Christians, primarily from laboring classes that were not at that time being reached by the church. He trained a large number of laymen as preachers who conducted preaching services and directed classes of instruction and of pastoral oversight.

The movement was transplanted to America where in pioneer times it spread quickly across the land by the preaching of circuit riders, most of whom were unmarried and able to live on very little salary. These early Methodists emphasized the importance of a definite experience of God's grace, a clear consciousness of their conversion, commitment to personal purity and integrity, and an enthusiasm for spreading the gospel. Bishop Francis Asbury was the great leader in early America, riding back and forth across the country from 1771 to 1816 for a total of some 270,000 miles, preaching 16,000 sermons, ordaining 4,000 ministers, and conducting 224 meetings of preachers.

During this same period two movements arose that eventually became the Evangelical United Brethren Church. One was the United Brethren in Christ, the other movement was originally called the Evangelical Association and later the Evangelical church. By 1946 these two groups merged to form the Evangelical United Brethren Church.

Divisions and Reunions

A sizeable group in the Methodist Episcopal Church, concerned about a more democratic church structure, withdrew from it in 1830 and formed the Methodist

Protestant Church. In 1844–45, the remaining members of the original Methodist body in this country divided into northern and southern branches, but these three segments came back together in 1939 as The Methodist Church.

By 1966 The Methodist Church and the Evangelical United Brethren church agreed to unite, and they did so in a General Conference in Dallas in 1968. Each church made certain concessions on their structure and practices, and each gained improvements from the other. The resulting denomination was called The United Methodist Church.

Approach to Faith

In the early days of America, Methodists sang: "I'd rather be a Methodist, with a round and shining face, than to be a long-faced Calvinist, that damns near half the race." Those lines, while hard on Calvinists, pointed toward the Methodist emphasis upon the love of God, a particular emphasis that is a very significant feature of Methodist history.

John Wesley preached that the grace and love of God are available to *all* people—not just a select few. He also declared that God gives to every person the ability to choose the good. All will be saved who turn to God in repentance, faith, and trust. Wesley had in his early years a life-changing experience that he described by saying, "I felt my heart strangely warm. I felt I did trust in Christ, Christ alone for salvation." This experience was stimulated, he said, at a meeting in which a part of Martin Luther's *Commentary on the Epistle to the Romans* had been read.

Wesley felt that it was wrong to hold that we have no responsibility at all for turning to God. He insisted that we have a role to play in salvation. The role involves using the ability of reason and emotion to *respond* to God's love and mercy, to *decide* to accept God's forgiveness, and to *trust* Jesus Christ as Lord and Savior. "Undoubtedly faith is the work of God," wrote Wesley, "and yet it is the duty of man to believe."

Understandings of God

United Methodists consider the core of the doctrine of the Trinity to be the affirmation of God as Father, as Son, and as Holy Spirit.

God the Creator shows loving care for all creatures. At the same time, God's judgment is real. If God is righteous, then sin and the tragic consequences of sin, individual and social, cannot be ignored. God suffers when we do wrong but does not reject us because mercy and grace are always a part of God's relationship with us.

United Methodists believe in Jesus Christ as Son of God and as Savior, Lord, and Master for all who accept his claim on their lives. Through Christ, God offers redemption to humankind, doing for us what we cannot do for ourselves, that is, bring new life and hope out of our shattered efforts.

God continues to be present within the church and within the life of the individual Christian through the Holy Spirit. The Holy Spirit is the Comforter, the Revealer of truth, and the Convictor of sin, bringing healing and purification. God's Spirit is ever active in the world and in the church—God will not be confined to certain historical dogmas. The Spirit breaks down every barrier and every formulation of the faith that would set itself up as the only true expression of the church.

Humankind and Salvation

United Methodists affirm that it is not possible for human beings to understand themselves apart from their relationship to God. True meaning and purpose in life are grounded only in God. Without this foundation, it is impossible to fulfill God's purposes. When human beings are alienated from God, they are captive to sin and turn away from God to many forms of cruelty, selfishness, and hardheadedness.

Methodists believe that human beings are responsible for their sins. People sin, not because of Adam or any first man, but because they do not want God's way but their own. While it is true that there are situations in life that are beyond human control, people are not robots. Human beings are creatures who must decide. Morality, Methodists would argue, is only possible in a situation where people have the choice between saying yes or no to worshiping God.

When people turn away from God in favor of their own selfish ends, only God can offer grace and forgiveness. Through Christ a person is able to see his or her own transgression. Through Christ's death and resurrection God does for people what they cannot do for themselves by bringing new life and hope.

Perfection in Christian Love

United Methodists believe that as Christians we can claim no merit because of what we do, but when God's love is within our hearts and lives, we will bring forth the fruits of faith—sometimes called "good works." We do not do good works to try to please God; we respond with good works because we love God and our fellow creatures. We cannot avoid showing our love in this way.

In their lives as Christians, United Methodists have followed—at least in theory—John Wesley's doctrine of Christian perfection. Wesley wrote: "Christian perfection is neither more nor less than pure love; love expelling sin, and governing both the heart and the life of the child of God." He believed that every Christian could experience this fullness of love. This doctrine has not always been at the forefront of Methodist teaching, but it is still part of the denomination's character.

Faith and Practice

Methodist churches give an important place to preaching the message of the Bible. Preaching is a means of witnessing to Christ or explaining the Christian faith, of bringing comfort and assurance to those under stress, and of confronting persons with challenge and rebuke when these are needed. In many United Methodist churches the sermon is considered the most important part of the worship service; however, it is increasingly considered one among several important aspects of worship.

There are two sacraments in United Methodist practice: Baptism and the Lord's Supper. People are made children of God through baptism. United Methodists allow any mode of baptism but usually practice sprinkling. They also practice infant baptism, believing that in it God declares through his church his love and concern for the child.

United Methodists believe in open communion; all are welcome who can honestly respond to the invitation to "truly and earnestly repent of your sins, and are in love and charity with your neighbors, and intend to lead a new life." They believe in the spiritual presence of Christ in the Lord's supper—as contrasted with the belief in a literal physical presence in the bread and wine.

Methodism looks to the Bible as the ground and guide of all Christian learning and living. Creeds are respected and are regularly used by United Methodists, but are not considered standards by which to test orthodoxy or as final statements for all ages. In official use are the Nicene Creed, the Apostles' Creed, two modern statements of faith, and the Confession of Faith of the former Evangelical United Brethren Church, prepared in 1946.

Social Concerns

The interest of United Methodists in all aspects of human life—personal and social—is based on the biblical concern for justice. This concern includes the poor and oppressed, the spiritual and physical welfare of all persons, and the need for peace and goodwill between people and nations.

This concern has been expressed for many years through the operation of hospitals, orphanages, social centers, homes for youth, and schools for those otherwise neglected. In more recent years, it has found additional expression in homes for older persons, in support of inner city churches and parishes, and in special ministries for minority groups.

The present statement of Social Principles in the *Book of Discipline* addresses a wide variety of issues including The Natural World, The Nurturing Community (family, sexuality), The Social Community (racial minorities, women, children, alcohol and other drugs, medical experimentation), The Economic Community, The Political Community, and The World Community.

In the Ecumenical Movement

The United Methodist Church, through the six original denominational strands that make up the present church, has a long history of involvement in the ecumenical movements of the twentieth century. One of the most important contributions has been in providing leadership through its pastors, bishops, and scholars. At another level, United Methodists always have carried a large responsibility for financial support of the many ecumenical activities in which they have participated, including projects of interdenominational cooperation such as the national Council of Churches of Christ and the World Council of Churches.

Features in Structure

The United Methodist Church is an episcopal body, which means that bishops appoint pastors to their churches. Individual United Methodist churches consider themselves as organic parts of the church as a whole—just as the various cells of one's physical body make up the body as a whole. The pastors of United Methodist churches are not members of the local churches they serve, but belong to one of the regional groups called annual conferences. There are five levels in the conference structure: *Charge Conference,* for the local church; *District,* under a superintendent, usually involving a dozen to forty churches; *Annual Conference,* with five to ten districts; *Jurisdictional Conference,* a large regional area made up of eight to twelve states, where bishops are elected; and *General Conference,* the highest legislative body, which meets every four years.

Composition of Membership

The United Methodist Church is found in almost every county in the nation. Its membership includes laborers, business executives, teachers, professional workers, salespersons, politicians; rich, poor, young, old. It includes a variety of races. Of all the predominantly white churches, it has the largest number of members who are black, native American, Hispanic, and Asian American. This diversity requires the members of United Methodist Churches to be open to cultural practices and outlooks which may be unfamiliar to them.

There is also a wide range of theological views among United Methodists. The denomination includes persons of conservative theological views and those of liberal views, and many in between. While individual believers may hold to their own theological convictions firmly, it is also important that members be tolerant of those who hold different beliefs. Similarly there is a broad spectrum of views among members on social issues—the use of natural resources, homosexuality, abortion, sexist language, God-language, welfare practices, and so on.

For Discussion

□ Do we have the ability, on our own, to turn toward God? Methodism would say yes, Lutheranism would say no. Which position would you favor?
□ Historically, Methodists have emphasized holy living more than have Lutherans. What do you think are the benefits and drawbacks of stressing such a lifestyle?
□ Methodists have been less willing than some other denominations to be tied down to historic statements of faith. Do you think this stance is an advantage or a liability?

For Further Study

□ *The People Called Methodist* by E. Gordon Rupp, et al. (Nashville: Discipleship Resources, 1984)
□ *Questions and Answers about the United Methodist Church* by Thomas S. McAnally (Nashville: Abingdon Press, 1995)
□ Methodist Web site: www.umc.org

Table of Comparison	*Methodists*	*Lutherans*
Teachings	1. Believe the Bible contains the Word of God; much disagreement here. 2. Teach justification by faith. 3. Consider Baptism and Holy Communion not only symbolically, but also as signs of God's grace. 4. Teach that all people have the ability to choose the good and turn to God. 5. Believe the church should express its faith in concrete action in the affairs of the world.	1. Accept the Bible as the written witness to God's revelation of saving action through Jesus Christ. 2. Same. 3. Consider Baptism and Holy Communion as God's means of conveying God's grace. 4. Teach that we can reject God, but it is only God's work that brings us to faith. 5. Believe the church lives to preach the Gospel and celebrate the sacraments, giving strength for service in the world.
Type of Worship	Formerly very free and emotional. Now moving toward more dignified and sometimes highly liturgical patterns.	Liturgical, following the classical forms of the Western Church.
Government	Episcopal, with bishop but no claim to apostolic succession. Congregations quite free within clearly defined channels.	Interdependent congregational, regional, national, and global expressions of the church characterized by democratic decision making, strong ecumenical relationships, elected leadership, and an ordained ministry.
Characteristics	Major emphasis on Christian living as the fruit of personal commitment and clear understanding of Christian doctrine. Leaders in movements for reunion of Christian communities of faith.	Strong emphasis on correct doctrine, with Christian life to proceed from belief as faith becomes active in love. Cautious about cooperation with other religious groups without doctrinal agreement.
Statistics*	Membership . . . . 8,495,378 Congregations . . . . 36,361 *United Methodist U. S. statistics from *Yearbook of American and Canadian Churches 1998*.	

CHAPTER 24

Moravian Church

The Moravian Church began when a Bohemian priest and scholar, John Hus, was burned at the stake at the Council of Constance in 1415.

The Moravian Church is not a large denomination. In spite of its small size, however, it is one of the few worldwide churches. Moravians claim that fellowship in Jesus Christ can transcend all differences, including those of political systems and skin color.

From earliest times, the Moravian Church has sought Protestant cooperation. Contact was made with Martin Luther during the German Reformation. At that time, there already were 175,000 Moravians. As a result of the contact, the Moravian Church, known as the *Unitas Fratrum* (Unity of Brethren), published its confession of faith with Luther writing the preface.

This spirit of cooperation continued in America. Moravian leaders in early Pennsylvania sought to encourage Protestant unity. Cooperation in this century can be seen in the fact that American Moravians were charter members of both the World and National Councils of Churches.

A Worldwide Unity

A unique quality of the Moravian Church is that it has maintained a worldwide Unity since the eighteenth century. Today's World Unity embraces nineteen independent provinces and missions located on every major continent except Australia.

The fastest growing segment of the worldwide Moravian Church today is found in Tanzania. The church is also present in South Africa, Suriname, Guyana, the West Indies, and Central America, as well as in Europe, the United Kingdom, and North America. There is also work among the native peoples of Alaska and Labrador. Each Unity province is an independent church, but a Unity Synod held every seven years provides overall coordination and direction for the church in the developed and the developing world.

Hus and Zinzendorf

The Moravian Church began when a Bohemian priest and scholar, John Hus, was burned at the stake at the Council of Constance in 1415. After efforts to purify the existing church failed, his followers were forced to organize their own body in 1457.

The Unity, as it was called, prospered for a time. It soon faced persecution, however, and seemed dead—but it was reborn. To a devout, pietistic, German Lutheran's estate in 1721 came a little band of refugees from Bohemia. Count Nicolaus von Zinzendorf permitted them to settle on his lands. Under Zinzendorf's leadership, they worshiped as Lutherans in the parish church. Other religiously dissatisfied people and refugees joined the community. But strife arose, and this community of Herrnhut seemed in danger of falling apart.

Count Zinzendorf abandoned his tasks at court and gave his full time to the community. He and the elders conducted a house-to-house visitation for prayer and study, which built toward a climax on August 13, 1727. The Brethren, gathered in the parish church, experienced an outpouring of God's Spirit of such vitality that the direction of the community was changed and it was formed into a solid base for spreading the gospel throughout the world.

From Europe the church spread to many parts of the world, seeking to take its message of Jesus to the forgotten people, such as the slaves and Indians in the Western Hemisphere. This pattern explains the fact that today the make up of the Moravian Church is about 80 percent black people, about 10 percent white people, and the remaining members are indigenous peoples.

Church and Sacraments

The Moravian Church recognizes the sacraments of Baptism and Holy Communion. The usual form of Baptism is sprinkling, and the church administers the sacrament in the name of the Triune God (Father, Son, and Holy Spirit). The sacrament carries with it the responsibility of parents, child, and congregation.

Baptism is a sign of God's love toward us even before we can understand it and a sign of our becoming part of the family of God through Christ. Baptized children may receive communion after some preparation; however, practice varies from congregation to congregation. A public profession of faith in Christ is made at the time of confirmation, or of adult baptism for someone who has not been baptized as an adult.

In the Moravian understanding of Holy Communion, the believer participates in the unique act of a covenant with Christ as Savior and with other believers in Christ. The Moravian service of Holy Communion is a service of praise and prayer (with hymns being sung as the elements are distributed to all communicants); of fellowship (with the right hand of fellowship extended at the beginning and close of the service); and of a special covenant with Christ and each other.

The Lovefeast

Moravian worship varies widely; freedom is intended. Liturgies, composed of prayers, scripture verses, and hymn stanzas, are provided for all occasions. The Moravian Easter Morning liturgy, sometimes called a Moravian confession of faith, draws heavily on Luther's Small Catechism. Another Moravian tradition is a series of services during Holy Week in which the entire Passion narrative of the gospels is read, interspersed with hymns. These liturgical forms are not intended to restrict creative expression on the part of any pastor or congregation.

A unique practice is the lovefeast, or the partaking of a simple meal in church. In such services, as in the service for Holy Communion, much of the message is in the words of the large number of hymns sung.

Christian Living

Moravians place a great stress on Christian living. This is not so much a listing of don'ts as it is an urging to live a life centered on Jesus Christ. The ideal Moravian is one who lives for Christ, rejoices in Christ, and whose life shows a spirit of love for others.

The Moravian Church emphasizes a warm experience of personal salvation and mission work. It sought to function within the state churches of Europe and to secure their support in taking the gospel abroad. It also witnessed the divisiveness of contrary doctrine. As a result, though conservative where the major doctrines (Trinity, and so forth) were concerned, it has consistently refused to define the fine points, such as what happens to the elements in the Holy Communion. Such definition is left to the individual Christian.

Broadly evangelical, the Moravians have insisted upon the principle of "in essentials unity, in non-essentials liberty, in all things love." The chief characteristic of its doctrinal approach came from Zinzendorf who said, "If I know Jesus, then I know all that I need to know about the Godhead."

Shape and Future

The ministry of the Moravian Church is grouped into three orders: deacon, presbyter, and bishop. The bishop is not a governmental figure but is chosen as a spiritual leader and pastor to pastors.

The future of the Moravian Church lies in its continued witness for Christ around the world. Growth in recent years has come mainly through immigration to the United States and Canada of Moravians from Central America and the Caribbean. Like many other Christians, Moravians need to learn how to witness to Jesus Christ in ways that people find meaningful and inviting.

For Discussion

□ Moravians and the Evangelical Lutheran Church in America are considering closer ties. Why would this seem to make sense?

□ The Moravians are a worldwide church. How does this compare with your denomination?

□ What are the benefits, and possible pitfalls, of the principle of "in essentials unity, in non-essentials liberty, in all things love"?

For Further Study

□ *All About the Moravians* by Edwin A. Sawyer (Bethlehem, Penn., and Winston-Salem, N. C., The Moravian Church in America, 1990)

□ *The Moravian Church through the Ages* by John R. Weinlick (Bethlehem, Penn., and Winston-Salem, N. C., The Moravian Church in America, 1989)

□ *Count Zinzendorf* by John R. Weinlick (Bethlehem, Penn., and Winston-Salem, N. C., The Moravian Church in America, 1989)

□ Moravian Web site: www.moravian.org

Table of Comparison	*Moravians*	*Lutherans*
Teachings	1. Accept major statements of faith of the early church as well as major confessions of Lutheran and Reformed traditions, including the Barmen Declaration of 1934, as valid expressions.	1. Accept the creeds, the Augsburg Confession, and Luther's Small Catechism as basic summaries of the faith. Recognize the remainder of the *Book of Concord* as valid interpretation of the faith of the Church.
	2. Great emphasis on Christ as the revelation of God.	2. Same.
	3. Affirm the inspiration of scripture, but much latitude here in interpretation.	3. Accept the Bible as the written witness to God's revelation of saving action through Jesus Christ.
	4. Baptism and Holy Communion are practiced but defined only in biblical terms. Each believer interprets those terms.	4. Baptism and Holy Communion are practiced as means of God's grace. Real presence of Christ in Communion affirmed.
	5. Believe in the necessity of individual regeneration and in salvation through Christ.	5. The baptized Christian lives in the covenant of his or her Baptism, dying to sin and rising again to faith in Christ.
Type of Worship	Semi-liturgical. Liturgies are available for every type of need but are not compulsory. Continue to celebrate lovefeast.	Liturgical, following the classic pattern of the Western church.
Government	"Conferential," with wide latitude given to congregations.	Interdependent congregational, regional, national, and global expressions of the church characterized by democratic decision making, strong ecumenical relationships, elected leadership, and an ordained ministry.
Characteristics	Major emphasis on Christian living as a result of Christian experience. Emphasis on individual interpretation of doctrine: "In essentials unity, in non-essentials liberty, in all things love." Leaders in all major movements for cooperation.	Christian living seen as an expression of Christian faith. Strong emphasis on doctrine. Increasingly involved in cooperative movements.
Statistics*	Membership . . . . 50,000 Congregations . . . . 160 *1996 U. S. statistics from the Moravian Church.	

CHAPTER 25

Presbyterian Church

The Presbyterian Church (U.S.A.) is the largest church body in the world with a presbyterian form of government. This body now has more than two and a half million members. But it is only one of many denominations that can properly be called *presbyterian,* since that word refers to a type of church organization common to a number of groups. This system of organization will be described later in this chapter.

The word presbyterian *indicates a form of organization and governance that is based upon rule by elected elders as representatives of the people.*

Tradition and Change

The Book of Confessions is the basic document of the Presbyterian confessional position. It contains the Nicene Creed, the Apostles' Creed, the Scots Confession, the Heidelberg Catechism, the Second Helvetic Confession, the Westminster Confession of Faith, the Shorter and Larger Catechisms, the Theological Declaration of Barmen, the Confession of 1967, and A Brief Statement of Faith. The adoption of the Book of Confessions indicates both a broad appreciation of the Presbyterian heritage and an effort to express the faith in ways that meet contemporary needs.

Presbyterian History

The presbyterian form of church organization was forged in the particular struggle to bring the Protestant Reformation to Geneva, Switzerland. The major insights of the Reformation had already been formulated by others, especially Martin Luther in Wittenberg, Germany, and Ulrich Zwingli in Zurich, Switzerland. John Calvin, the spiritual father of Presbyterians, was only eight years old when Luther nailed his 95 Theses to the church door in Wittenberg. The great principles of the Reformation, such as the authority of Scripture, the right of private judgment, justification by faith, the sanctity of common life, and the mutual ministry of all believers, were a part of the legacy Calvin inherited from Luther, Zwingli, and others.

Calvin and Knox

John Calvin (1509–1564) was born in France and trained as a lawyer. When he came to Geneva, the Reformation had already begun there, but much work remained. Calvin was a gifted thinker, and already at age 26 he wrote *The*

Institutes of the Christian Religion, a work that remains influential today. After his arrival in Geneva, Calvin's already considerable reputation as a biblical scholar and theologian continued to grow. As a result, the city became at once a theological center of the Reformation and a haven for persecuted Protestants from other countries.

One of the most distinguished refugees was the fiery Scot, John Knox (ca. 1514–1572). As pupil and assistant to Calvin, Knox was preparing himself for eventual return to his native Scotland and a confrontation with its Roman Catholic queen, Mary. At this time, England and Scotland were separate countries. While Mary professed allegiance to Rome and the Catholic faith, England had already rejected its allegiance to the pope. The ensuing struggle between the two countries was bitter, but Knox succeeded in reforming the Church of Scotland, and Mary's son, James (after whom the King James Version of the Bible is named) became Protestant king of the united countries of England and Scotland following the death of Elizabeth I of England.

Into America

Presbyterianism was carried to America by a variety of immigrants—Dutch, English, Scottish, French, Swiss, and others. Congregations were established from New England to the Carolinas, but particularly in the middle colonies.

Presbyterians played a prominent role in the colonies' struggle for independence. John Witherspoon, a minister from Scotland who came to America to be president of the College of New Jersey (later known as Princeton University), was the only clergyperson and one of several Presbyterians to sign the Declaration of Independence.

The Civil War and several major theological controversies created a number of splits in the ranks of American Presbyterianism. Since 1865, however, a number of unions have taken place. Notable among these was the union in 1958 between the United Presbyterian Church of North America and the Presbyterian Church in the United States of America that produced the largest Presbyterian group up to that time, The United Presbyterian Church in the United States of America. In 1983 this group unified with the former "Southern" Presbyterians to form the Presbyterian Church (U.S.A.).

Theological Concern

There are no real novelties in Presbyterian doctrine. Presbyterians are trinitarian Christians standing in the mainstream of Western reformed tradition. This does not mean that there are no distinctions between Presbyterian beliefs about basic doctrine and those beliefs held by other Protestant religious bodies, but such differences tend to be matters of accent and emphasis rather than of fundamental disagreement.

An illustration of a particular emphasis may be seen in the Presbyterian teaching about God. *Sovereignty* is a good word to summarize this teaching. It implies an exalted concept of God as creator of the universe, as the sustainer of all God has made, and as sole ruler of all things natural, human, and historical. If other churches, such as the Methodists, stress the love of God and the warmhearted response of the believer, Presbyterians may be said to stress the righteousness of God and humanity's duty to obey.

The *Shorter Catechism,* a part of Presbyterian confessional statements for more than 300 years, asks in its first question: "What is the chief end of man?" The answer: "To glorify God and enjoy him forever." Perhaps no other two sentences are more typically Presbyterian.

Sin and Hope

It is typical of Presbyterian thought to regard the sinful nature of humanity with stark realism. An often misunderstood phrase that belongs to this tradition is "total depravity." It does not mean that everything one thinks or wills or does is only evil. Rather, it means that sin corrupts all our faculties so that none of them serve God perfectly. In God's eyes, therefore, even our best thoughts and deeds are never wholly pure.

Presbyterians have been accused of painting too bleak a picture of human nature. They are not pessimists, however, for they believe in a God who is not only righteous, but merciful as well. The gospel is *good news*. That good news is not try harder to be better. Indeed, that would be bad news. Rather the good news is that God loves sinners. God does not condemn us for being what we are. God calls upon us to confess our sin and trust God's grace. When we do so, the burden of guilt is lifted and we are empowered to do that which by our own strength was previously impossible.

Presbyterians as a whole have been a people who have taken their duties seriously, who have tried to be righteous, moral, and diligent in the common walks of life. The purpose of such living is not to win God's favor, which has already been fully and freely given, but to express gratitude in lives that will be well-pleasing to God.

Signs of the Church

With the churches of the Reformation, Presbyterians hold that the true church is found where the gospel is truly preached and heard, where the sacraments are faithfully administered and received, and where due discipline enables the ministry of Word and sacrament to occur.

This understanding means that the Presbyterian church does not claim to be the whole church, but only a part of the universal, visible church on earth. It seeks cooperation and fellowship with others who acknowledge Jesus Christ as Lord, as can be seen in its work in the Consultation on Church Union. It is committed to ecumenicity and interprets its global mission as one of partnership and sharing with others around the world in doing the work of Jesus Christ.

The *Book of Order* of the reunited Presbyterian church lays a strong and specific emphasis upon the inclusiveness and global nature of the church. This emphasizes the Presbyterian concern for people of all ages, races, cultures, sexes, and conditions, wherever they may live. It calls for dialogue with and respect for those of religious persuasions that are other than Christian. It means standing with the oppressed, economically, politically, or religiously, and working for their freedom in justice.

Preaching and Worship

Historically, preaching has been emphasized in the Presbyterian church. The pulpit and Bible are often central in its architecture. The proclamation of the Word rightly includes teaching as well as preaching, reflecting the conviction that preparation of persons to hear the Word is as important as its declaration. Presbyterians have therefore been deeply involved in education of all kinds, including the founding and support of many colleges, universities, and seminaries here and around the world.

Among Presbyterian constitutional documents is the *Directory for Worship*. This document sets out standards and practices for worship but does not require that these be followed. *Sessions* (local governing bodies) are given freedom regarding the form and order of worship in the congregation. As a result, wide variations occur in practice.

Sacraments: Baptism and the Lord's Supper

Two sacraments are affirmed by the Presbyterian church—Baptism and the Lord's Supper. In the Presbyterian tradition infants as well as adults are baptized. The congregation and the parents have a "special obligation" to lead the baptized person to "a personal response to the love of God," according to the Confession of 1967.

The Lord's Supper was long a point of separation between the Presbyterian and Reformed churches and the Lutheran churches. The differences had to do chiefly with how Christ was seen as present in the sacrament, whether his presence was "spiritual" or "real." Recent ecumenical discussions, however, have found these differences to be matters more of nuance than substance, and large segments of the two traditions now affirm each other's sacramental understanding as being valid.

Authority of Scripture

The use of the Bible among Presbyterians deserves special mention. Perhaps no subject has stirred more controversy within the Presbyterian camp. All agree that the Word of God is of highest significance. But all do not agree as to what the Word of God is, or how it is to be interpreted. Some Presbyterians equate the Word of God with the words of scripture, and make assertions of inerrancy and infallibility in a restricted and literal sense. Others advocate a broader and older view, recognizing Jesus Christ as the Word Incarnate, the one sufficient revelation of God. The Confession of 1967 declares, "The church has received the books of the Old and New Testaments as prophetic and apostolic testimony in which it hears the Word of God and by which its faith and obedience are nourished and regulated."

Presbyterian Order

If Presbyterians may be said to be passionate about anything it might well be their desire to do all things "decently and in order." The very word *presbyterian* comes from the Greek word for "elder" and indicates a form of organization and governance that is based upon rule by elected elders as representatives of the people. For many years the presbyterian system has recognized three offices in the church, which are ordained after election by the people: elders, deacons, and ministers of the Word and Sacrament. Ordination to these three offices is the same, although the requirements for them may differ, as do their functions in the church.

The presbyterian form, then, differs from the episcopal form in which power is vested in a person (bishop), and the congregational form where power is vested in the people. Presbyterian government is representative, not hierarchical or purely democratic. Authority in the presbyterian system resides in a system of interconnected "governing bodies."

The congregation is ruled by the *Session* made up of elders elected by the people with the pastor as Moderator (presiding officer). This body is responsible for the life and work of the congregation—its worship, education, program, and mission. It makes policy and decides issues.

The *Presbytery* is a representative body composed of the ministers of the Word and Sacrament who serve congregations within its bounds, and elder representatives from each congregation within the geographical area of the presbytery. The presbytery performs the responsibilities of a bishop: ordaining and installing ministers of the Word and Sacrament in congregations; overseeing the work of the congregations; judging disputes; providing services to the churches that they could not provide separately; and interpreting to the congregations the work of the whole church. Ministers of the Word and Sacrament are members of the presbytery, not of congregations, and the consent of the presbytery is required for a change in the terms of their call to serve a particular congregation or for a change in location of their pastoral services.

The *Synod* is a regional body, often encompassing several states. It has responsibility for the presbyteries within its bounds and helps to provide services that the individual presbyteries could not provide.

The most inclusive governing body is the *General Assembly*. This body is made up of an equal number of ministers and elders elected by the presbyteries. It meets at least every two years to debate denominational policy, to hear appeals, and to recommend programs, strategies, and resources for the life of the denomination.

Seeking New Ways

The Presbyterian Church (U.S.A.) has an openness to change; a concern to cooperate with others in attempting to be faithful to the larger church of which it is a part; the courage to venture and to disagree; a commitment to social justice and inclusiveness; and a willingness to risk, particularly when working in secular realms where the prophetic voice of the church may not be welcome. There is much in its life to criticize, and critics are not lacking. It is a church that is seeking always to be reformed and recognizes that it is always in need of reform. It seeks earnestly for new ways to fulfill Christ's mission for our time.

For Discussion

- □ Which confessions do we and the Presbyterians have in common? How important are such documents?
- □ What similarities and differences do you see between our beliefs and those of the Presbyterian church?
- □ What do you see as the strengths of the presbyterian form of church organization?

For Further Study

All of the following are available from the Presbyterian Publishing Corporation, 1-800-227-2872.

- □ *How to Spell Presbyterian* by James W. Angell
- □ *To Be a Presbyterian* by Louis B. Weeks
- □ *Book of Order*
- □ *Book of Confessions*
- □ Presbyterian Church U.S.A. Web site: www.pcusa.org

Table of Comparison	*Presbyterians*	*Lutherans*
Teachings	1. Bible regarded as the "witness without parallel" to Jesus Christ who is the one sufficient revelation of God. 2. Accept Nicene and Apostles' Creeds, the Scots Confession, the Heidelberg Catechism, the Second Helvetic Confession, the Westminster Confession and the Shorter Catechism, the Theological Declaration of Barmen, and the Confession of 1967. 3. Consider the sacraments as visible signs of an invisible grace, confirming our faith in the proclaimed Word. 4. Believe that in Communion the body and blood of Christ are really present, but received spiritually.	1. Bible regarded as the written witness to God's revelation of saving action through Jesus Christ. 2. Accept Nicene and Apostles' Creeds as well as the Augsburg Confession and Luther's Small Catechism. Book of Concord basic collection of doctrinal documents of the Reformation era. 3. Consider the sacraments as actual channels of God's grace to us. 4. Believe that the communicant receives Christ's body and blood in, with, and under the bread and wine.
Type of Worship	Varies from liturgical to free, usually with sermon as the climax.	Liturgical with both Word and sacrament together making a complete service.
Government	Ruled by a series of courts in which elders elected by the people share authority with the ministers. There are four levels of church courts.	Interdependent congregational, regional, national, and global expressions of the church characterized by democratic decision making, strong ecumenical relationships, elected leadership, and an ordained ministry.
Characteristics	Major concern for the church's work in facing the needs of society. In practice, leavened bread and grape juice used in Communion. Distributed to worshipers in the pews.	Not as active in social involvement, but faith to be practiced in life. Unleavened or leavened bread and wine used in Communion. Elements received by communicants at the chancel.
Statistics*	Membership . . . . 2,609,191 Congregations . . . . 11,295 *Statistics from Presbyterian Church (U. S. A.)	

CHAPTER 26

Reformed Church in America

In the Reformed Church infants are baptized as heirs of the covenant of grace.

The Reformed Church in America is the oldest Protestant church in America with an uninterrupted ministry. The Dutch who settled New Amsterdam (now New York) organized the first Reformed Church on this continent in 1628. Although the English took over the area in 1664 and English became the language of the land, the Reformed Church continued to use the Dutch language for nearly a century.

Both historically and theologically, the Reformed Church in America stands in the Calvinist tradition of the Protestant Reformation. But it does not have the rigidity that has characterized some churches in that tradition. It combines the doctrine of God's sovereignty with a warm evangelical doctrine of Christ and a strong witness to the power of the Holy Spirit.

The church is seen as the body of believers in Christ and their children. Two sacraments are practiced: Baptism and the Lord's Supper. Both are viewed as means of grace, signs and seals of God's covenant of grace with us.

Infants are baptized as heirs of the covenant of grace. In this act, they are officially incorporated into the life of the Christian church. In regard to the Lord's Supper, the Reformed Church speaks of the presence of Christ in the elements of bread and wine in Holy Communion.

The Bible is confessed to be the Word of God, inspired by God and written by human beings. The authority and infallibility of the Bible extends over all that God intends to say to us in it and all that the Bible intends to teach. Reformed Churches also subscribe to the Heidelberg Catechism, a sixteenth century document relating to Christian life and witness.

The way of worship is neither completely regulated nor completely free. Required liturgical forms are provided for the sacraments. In government, the presbyterian pattern is followed. Local congregations are governed by a consistory, made up of the pastor and elected elders and deacons. A *classis* oversees the congregations in a local jurisdiction, and in turn reports to one of seven regional synods. A General Synod is the churchwide policy maker.

The Reformed Church, generally, is an ecumenically minded denomination. It has been a member of both the National Council of Churches and the World Council of Churches since each was started and is included in the Formula of Agreement between various Reformed denominations and the Evangelical Lutheran Church in America.

For Discussion

□ In terms of how language shaped the church in the United States, what similarities do you see between the Reformed Church and the Lutheran church?

□ An emphasis on God's sovereignty is central for Reformed Churches; Luther and his followers preferred to emphasize the cross of Christ. What strengths does each bring to the Christian life?

For Further Study

□ *Flourishing in the Land* by Scott Hoezee and Christopher Meehan (Grand Rapids: Eerdmans, 1996)

□ Reformed Church Web site: www.crcna.org

Table of Comparison	*Reformed Church*	*Lutherans*
Teachings	1. Accept Bible as the Word of God. 2. Trinitarian. Believe in the deity and humanity of Christ and accent both. 3. Justification by God's grace, accepted by faith. 4. Celebrate two sacraments: Baptism and Holy Communion. Consider them means of grace; speak of the presence of Christ in the Lord's Supper.	1. Accept the Bible as the written witness to God's revelation of saving action through Jesus Christ. 2. Same. 3. Justification by grace through faith proclaimed. 4. Celebrate two sacraments: Baptism and Holy Communion. Consider them means of grace; affirm the real presence of Christ in the Lord's Supper.
Type of Worship	Worship in semi-liturgical; for the sacraments, forms are fixed; great freedom in other parts of the church's worship.	Liturgical, following classic traditions and services of the Western church. Preaching of the Word and celebration of sacrament main events of worship.
Government	Presbyterian pattern used with representative church government. The church ruled by elders with clergy considered teaching elders.	Interdependent congregational, regional, national, and global expressions of the church characterized by democratic decision making, strong ecumenical relationships, elected leadership, and an ordained ministry.
Characteristics	Seek balance between a strong emphasis on doctrine and the demands of Christian responsibility to transform culture in accordance with Christ's commands. Ecumenically minded.	Emphasis on doctrine, with Christian practice supposed to proceed from faith in Christ. Ecumenically aware, but historically cautious about cooperative movements.
Statistics*	Membership .... 304,113 Congregations .... 909 *U. S. statistics from *Yearbook of American and Canadian Churches 1998.*	

CHAPTER 27

Religious Society of Friends

Friends believe that God can speak to anyone directly. Their meetings for worship are open for anyone to stand up and speak or pray.

Perhaps when we hear Quakers mentioned, a mental picture of the smiling plump face beneath a dark broad-brimmed hat flashes into mind. Quakers are often associated with a quaint, old-fashioned people who came with William Penn centuries ago to found the colony of Pennsylvania.

Today's modern Quakers have left this image in the past. Instead of being an old-fashioned sect that would appear more comfortable in an early American museum, modern Quakers (or Friends) are very much in tune with many of today's religious changes. Drawing on their tradition, they want to reduce to a minimum any distinctions between clergy and laity; they have given equal recognition and responsibilities to men and women, including the ministry; they have pioneered in bringing constructive alternatives to social injustices and human exploitation; they have found genuine Christian fellowship more readily in small informal groups working and worshiping together; they have cherished a freedom to express their convictions without being boxed in by creeds and ritual.

They are, however, still a small group. It's not easy to be a Quaker because their convictions often differ from popular attitudes about militarism, gambling, and personal moral behavior. To be a Quaker calls for a higher degree of individual responsibility, initiative, and integrity than many church members are ready to give.

Four Major Groups

Quakers in America today are divided into various groups as a result of theological controversies. The Friends United Meeting includes about half the Friends in the world. It represents an orthodox theological position. The second group is the Friends General Conference which represents a more liberal theological position. A third body is the Evangelical Friends International, taking a more fundamentalist view, and a fourth is the Religious Society of Friends (Conservative). Both Friends United Meeting and Evangelical Friends engage in extensive foreign mission work.

Today's Quaker younger adults and youth are ready for more changes in order to have their faith deal more directly with the human needs that confront us all. They have been participating more in ecumenical activities with neighboring churches and in councils of churches; however, no serious merger discussions are under way with other denominations.

Founder: George Fox

Are Quakers and Friends the same? Yes, they take their name *Friends* from Jesus' words, "You are my friends if you do what I command you" (John 15:14). The term *Quaker* came about because their founder, George Fox, once scolded a judge for an unfair sentence by saying he should quake (tremble) before the Lord for handing out such a sentence as an example of justice.

Fox was a young man who did not like what he saw continuing in the name of the church in his day. He lived in England in the seventeenth century. It was a time of great religious and political turmoil. To some, the established church seemed to substitute rituals for inward religious experience and personal integrity. As a result, some people were dissatisfied and began seeking a religion of genuine personal experience in direct communion with God. Fox was among these seekers. He went to clergymen for help and received such advice as to have some blood drained, to chew tobacco, and to get married in order to find inner peace of mind. After these disappointments, he sought help directly from God. It came to him in a profound religious experience in which he heard a voice within saying, "There is one, even Christ Jesus, who can speak to thy condition." He was elated to find the way to direct communion with God.

Fox was 23 years old when he began preaching in great joy of his discovery that Christ was available to be any person's teacher. This was a revolutionary discovery for his day, and he soon ran into strong opposition. Thousands of Friends were jailed and their property taken. They were persecuted (hundreds died in prison and several were hanged) because they would not conform to their country's religious and political establishments.

Because of the persecution, great numbers of early Friends came to America to enjoy religious and political freedom. Not only was Pennsylvania a Quaker stronghold, but the colonies of Rhode Island, New Jersey, Maryland, and North Carolina also had large Quaker populations and were ruled by Quaker governors with Quaker majorities in their early representative bodies. By the time Fox died in 1691 there were nearly 50,000 Friends in England, Europe, and colonial America. In this country, largely through the work of John Woolman, all Quakers freed their slaves some 70 years before the Civil War.

Theology: Faith to Work

Friends hold many beliefs in common with other Christian denominations; however, they have not placed as much stress on theology as upon putting their faith to work. Emphasis is placed upon the contemporary Spirit of Christ as productive to growing Christian faith. Friends have sometimes described the contemporary Christ living within the person of faith as the *Light within*. Salvation is seen as a process of obedient living that begins with a conscious commitment to be a follower of Christ.

Friends believe that every person is born with an inner capacity to respond to God's Spirit without having a minister to act as a go-between. Friends describe this capacity to be responsive as "that of God in every one." No person, even if he or she has never heard about Jesus, is left stranded without hope of knowing

God and responding to God's love. Although Friends are optimistic about a person's capacity to do good, they believe everyone has to accept God's redemptive, loving Spirit into his or her life before the tenacious power of sin or the haunting fear of death can be overcome. Once the inward Light of Christ is a part of a person's life, though, it will result in peace, integrity, equality, and community.

Although most Friends support the doctrine of the Trinity, they prefer to focus attention upon God's action in the world rather than formulating a statement about God's nature. There are some liberal Friends who prefer a unitarian interpretation to the trinitarian interpretation.

Church: People in Fellowship

The church is a people of God called into fellowship, worship, and service in order to make God's love known in this world. Friends have used the word *church* only to describe the fellowship of believers. The local congregation is called a Meeting and their place of worship is a meeting house. They describe their weekly services as meetings for worship, when they come together to meet in the presence of Christ. They call themselves a Religious Society of Friends instead of a church because they do not believe even good people can create the church, only God can do this.

They rely upon the scriptures as inspired and as one of the primary channels of God's revealed truth, but not the exclusive revelation of truth. A small number of Friends hold to a literalistic interpretation of the Bible. Quakers believe in the continuing revelation of truth through the inspiration of the Holy Spirit.

Friends do not use creeds, holding that all believers should be free to describe their own convictions on the basis of their own religious experience rather than using the words of someone else. Although this allows considerable freedom, there are carefully prepared questions that all Friends are to use for periodic self-examination to see if they are faithfully participating in the movement of Friends.

No Sacraments

Friends do not observe any of the traditional sacraments. They believe that all of life is sacred, not just special days, persons, or rituals. They believe in the inward baptism of the Spirit as the heart of personal religious experience, but that the ceremony of using water is not essential. They believe in the communion of a worshiping congregation with the Spirit of the risen Christ, but that it is not necessary to use the outward symbols of bread and wine to participate in this experience. Friends assert that none of these ceremonies was explicitly taught by Jesus as ritual.

Ministry and Worship

The Friends' view of ministry and worship differs from traditional Protestant views. They believe that all believers are called to be ministers by using their spiritual gifts. Believing that God can speak to anyone directly, their meetings for worship are open for anyone to stand up and speak or pray as he or she may feel inspired by the Spirit of Christ.

The traditional meeting for worship proceeds without a preplanned order of service. The worshipers gather quietly in the meeting room and consciously turn their minds to prayer and meditation. Elders sit at the front, facing the congregation, and are responsible for maintaining the quiet dignity of the meeting. Should anyone take advantage of this freedom to participate by speaking in a way that is obviously not in the spirit of worship, an elder may gently interrupt and ask the speaker to sit down.

A majority of the American Friends Meetings now use pastors. The Friends pastor, who may be a man or a woman, carries out many of the same functions as a Protestant clergyperson, but there are some distinct differences. He or she leaves time in the meetings of worship for others to participate. Occasionally the pastor may not speak at all if he or she does not feel truly inspired. The primary role of the pastor is to detect the undeveloped spiritual gifts in others and to help each member more fully employ them. The pastor sees himself or herself as part of a team ministry in partnership with other gifted members.

The local Meeting (congregation) is the basic governing body in the Religious Society of Friends, subject to the authority of the regional Yearly Meeting. All the members may participate in the monthly business meeting presided over by a clerk. There is no voting; decisions are reached only when the whole body is persuaded that they are in obedient response to the leading of the Spirit.

Peacemakers

Friends have throughout their history worked at being peacemakers by both binding up the wounds of war in relief services and by trying to remove the causes of war. They believe it is evil to kill another human being under any circumstance because every person is a child of God. They believe in the use of restraint and police force to protect the innocent and to provide the opportunity to transform the aggressor into a useful, responsible citizen.

This same conviction of the Friends concerning the sacredness of all life has made them leaders in movements to eliminate racial discrimination and to improve the care for the mentally retarded and for prisoners. They have worked to secure the rights of American Indians and other minority groups.

The American Friends Service Committee is widely known for its peacemaking and social reform services. It is an independent agency under the direction of a Quaker board. In all of the Friends' involvement in the community and world, they are trying to give faithful expression to their religious life and experience to make their contribution toward God's kingdom among humankind.

For Discussion

□ Friends emphasize right living over right belief. What are the advantages and dangers of such an approach?

□ Martin Luther warned against those who looked for individual revelation rather than finding God in the Bible or the church. Do you think that such concerns are justified?

□ Compare the Quaker tradition of pacifism with the approach of your church.

For Further Study

□ *Guide to Quaker Practice* by Howard Brinton (Wallingford, Penn.: Pendle Hill, 1993)

□ *Living Faith: An Historical Study of Quaker Beliefs* by Wilmer Cooper (Richmond, Ind.: Friends United Press, 1990)

□ *Quaker Spirituality: Selected Writings* ed. Douglas V. Steere (Mahwah, N.J.: Paulist Press, 1984)

□ Quaker Web page: www.quaker.org

Table of Comparison	*Quakers*	*Lutherans*
Teachings	1. Accept the Scriptures as inspired, but not exclusive revelation of truth. 2. Believe in Christ as Lord and Savior. 3. Teach responsible obedience to leading of Holy Spirit. 4. Do not consider traditional sacraments as necessary to salvation. 5. Believe that the sacredness of all human life does not allow anyone to exploit or destroy another.	1. Accept the Scriptures as the written witness to God's revelation of saving action through Jesus Christ. 2. Same. 3. Same. 4. Sacraments of Baptism and Holy Communion considered channels of God's grace for the salvation of humankind. 5. Historically grant the need for law and force in governing all people on earth. Such an attitude admits the possible necessity of war.
Type of Worship	Informal with simplicity and dignity in only a minimum of prearranged order. Worshipers may speak or pray as they feel inspired. Some meetings presided over by a pastor who shares with others in the ministry.	Liturgical forms used for the sake of good order. People involved in dialog of liturgical worship led by pastor, who is trained and called to the public office of the ministry on behalf of the people.
Government	Local Meeting (congregation) is autonomous. All members may participate in monthly business meetings presided over by a clerk. There is no voting. Relationship to large bodies through representation and recommendation, not by centralized control.	Interdependent congregational, regional, national, and global expressions of the church characterized by democratic decision making, strong ecumenical relationships, elected leadership, and an ordained ministry.
Characteristics	Major emphasis on Christian living and reconciliation; little stress on doctrine. Pioneers in peacemaking and social reforms.	Doctrine considered important with faith to be made active in love. Involved in social aid and relief, but historically hesitant about social involvement in issues of society and government.
Statistics*	Membership . . . . 189,466 Congregations . . . . 2,472 *U. S. statistics from *Yearbook of American and Canadian Churches 1998.*	

CHAPTER 28

Roman Catholic Church

The Catholic church recognizes the pope as the successor of Peter and chief teacher and shepherd of the church.

Many of the church bodies discussed in this book trace their roots back to the Roman Catholic Church. Those who have studied the history of the Reformation may be aware of the problems that led to those divisions, but the Catholic church today is a much different institution.

The transition to modern Catholicism began in the nineteenth century. Already then, Catholic theologians were beginning to look closer into the biblical nature of the church as the body of Christ, his living presence in the world. Several forces of change, including biblical, theological, liturgical, and social movements, prepared the Catholic church and its members for the updating of the church. All this preparation bore fruit in the mid–twentieth century in a very important worldwide church council commonly called Vatican II.

The Second Vatican Council was a council of reform. This reform was not aimed so much at correcting obvious abuses, as existed at the time of Martin Luther; rather, the Council sought a renewal of the very idea of religious practice, belief, and worship. Since then, these concepts have been brought to reality under the guidance of vigorous leaders such as Pope Paul VI and Pope John Paul II.

Foundation of the Church

It is the belief of Catholics that the Roman church grew out of Jesus' formation of the apostles into a community. Through this community he would continue to teach and sanctify people until the end of time.

From among the apostles Jesus chose Peter (the name means "rock") to be the solid foundation for his church, the one who would, in a sense, take the Lord's own place when he would leave this world. This is one Catholic interpretation of Matthew 16:16–20. Catholics further believe that Jesus confirmed his choice of Peter after the resurrection when he told Peter, "Feed my lambs . . . tend my sheep" (John 21:15–18).

After presiding over the church at Jerusalem and Antioch for some years, Peter went to Rome as the first "bishop" of the Christian community in that city. Catholic teaching claims that the future bishops of Rome have succeeded to the office of Peter as the chief teacher and shepherd of the church, the one whose main task is to "strengthen your brothers" (Luke 22:32).

The growth of the church over the centuries since its founding has been both human and divine. It has grown numerically and in depth, penetrating the mass of humankind with the mind of Christ. At the same time, it has been subject to human weaknesses and has experienced years and at times long periods of corruption. Catholics believe, however, that despite all the defects of the members of the church and even popes, the promise of Jesus has been maintained, that the powers of death have not prevailed against it, nor will they.

Mystery of God

In common with most Christian denominations, the Roman Catholic Church believes in the doctrine of the Trinity, taught by Jesus as the keystone of the new revelation. The Trinity is a "mystery." It could not have been known by humans without divine revelation. And even with the revelation, it cannot be wholly understood. But simply stated, the doctrine of the Trinity means that one God exists in three "persons." The three persons share one divine nature and therefore are equally eternal and almighty.

The Father is described in the gospels as one who guides and watches over his children, forgives them when they stray, and cares for them in all their needs. He is also the great king who watches over the earth. In Jesus, the Son of God, God becomes visible. The Son became human; that is, he became like us in all things except sin. Dying on the cross and rising from death, Jesus restores the possibility of living forever with God. The Holy Spirit is the personification, the making real, of the mutual love between the Father and the Son, and is the life principle of the body of Christ, the church. It is the Spirit who gives us a taste for God and God's Word and who makes us capable of living in love. The Spirit is responsible for the urge among Christians to come together in unity.

Salvation from God

The Catholic church believes that Jesus is the only savior of humankind. Salvation is the free gift of God that can in no way be merited by any human work. Humankind, which in some mysterious way was cut off from God and immersed in evil, is restored in Christ by his saving word and deed—his entire life, death, and resurrection.

Although everyone is considered a member of redeemed humanity, the Catholic church teaches that simple membership in the church does not automatically imply salvation. Each person is responsible for his or her own life and the manner in which he or she responds to Christ. As Jesus often warned, it is possible for anyone to be lost, to choose eternal separation from God and from fellowship in God's people.

Even though some Catholics (like other Christians) may give the impression that they think they can *work out their own salvation* by following rules and laws, performing religious rites and practicing self-denial, it is the authentic teaching of the Catholic church that it is Christ alone who saves. The person's only task is to accept that salvation with loving trust.

The Church: God's People

Despite how it may appear at times, the church is not at heart simply an organization, but the mystery of the People of God. Its purpose is to bear witness to Christ and to be Christ to the nations.

As the humanity of Christ is the sacrament, the effective sign, the manifestation of the Father, so the church is the sacrament of Christ. And the sacraments in turn are the manifestation, the showing forth, of the church. As Christ acted upon people by word and deed during his life on earth, so he now acts through the sacraments in the church that, as Pope Leo pointed out in the fifth century, are the extension of his humanity.

The task of bishops and priests is to be Christ to their people—to proclaim his Word and to bring the very life of God by means of the sacraments. Above all, they are to preside over the Eucharist—Holy Communion—so that the people may personally enter into Christ's redeeming work and make it their own.

Sacraments: Sacred Signs

The sacraments are sacred signs of spiritual strength, healing, and food whereby Jesus enters personally into the lives of Christians. By the power of Christ, sacraments accomplish what they signify. For instance, Baptism is the sign of cleansing and dying with Christ in order to rise with him, and through Christ's power that dying and rising becomes real. The Eucharist not only indicates food and nourishment, but it also provides spiritual food, the body and blood of Jesus, the bread of life.

The sacraments accompany human living, bringing God's grace to bear at various points in life. *Baptism* can be seen as corresponding to birth or adoption into a human family or becoming a naturalized citizen. It is becoming a member of the family of God. *Confirmation* functions as a bridge between Baptism and the Eucharist, as the maturing Christian moves deeper into the faith. *Penance* meets the needs of a person who falls into sin; Christ heals the sinner and restores him or her to healthy membership with the people of God. *Eucharist* corresponds to the need of every human being for food on the journey of life. And in any serious illness, in a person's most desperate need, Christ comes to him or her in the Sacrament of the *Anointing of the Sick* to strengthen and comfort—and often to restore the sick person to health. Finally, there are two sacraments—*Matrimony* and *Orders*—in which the recipient gives oneself in service. In Matrimony, Christ enters into the lives of husbands and wives, joins them in love for one another and for him, and gives them courage and help necessary to be faithful to their difficult vocation. And in Orders, Jesus chooses men, even as he chose the apostles, to do what he has done: "As the Father has sent me, so I send you" (John 20:21).

The Mass

The primary worship service of the Roman Catholic Church is called the Mass. It has two parts, the Liturgy of the Word and the Liturgy of the Eucharist. In the Liturgy of the Word, the assembly focuses upon God's Word through hearing and responding to readings from the Bible, prayers of petition and praise, and the homily. The Liturgy of the Word prepares the people for the second part of the Mass, the Liturgy of the Eucharist, which includes prayers of praise and thanksgiving, offering, petition, and remembrance. Its heart is the recital by the priest, speaking in the name of the assembly, of the Eucharistic Prayer, which includes an account of the Last Supper. Then those present who wish to do so receive Jesus as food for their souls, and for their daily living in their families and communities.

Pope and Bishops

Since Vatican II, the idea of collegial, or shared authority, has come more and more to the fore. We see this model at work in all these situations: pope and bishops gathered in "general councils" such as Vatican II; the Synod of Bishops elected by national governing groups around the world meeting regularly with the pope as a kind of senate to discuss problems relating to beliefs and practices of Catholics; diocesan (area) synods of priests helping their bishops shepherd, serve, and teach the faithful; parish councils of laity chosen by fellow parishioners helping the pastor with the spiritual and temporal administration of the parish.

It is Catholic belief that among the bishops the pope holds special duties and privileges. One of the chief functions of the pope is that of teacher. He is the head of the College of Bishops and therefore possesses in a special measure divine protection from teaching error. By this infallibility, Catholics do not believe that the pope is incapable of sinning or of erring in matters other than doctrine. Infallibility is not a personal quality of the pope. It belongs to his office and is only for the benefit of the people of God.

Points of Difference

This concept of authority in the church, centering in the papacy, probably distinguishes Catholics from Protestants more than any other doctrine. It is often the least understood teaching.

Another point of difference has to do with the Virgin Mary. It is a Catholic belief that Mary was a virgin *before, during,* and *after* the birth of her son Jesus, though the "before" is stressed more than the "during and after." The "brothers and sisters" of Jesus mentioned in the Gospels are thought to have been his relatives, not his blood brothers and sisters, for the word *brothers* in Aramaic can also be used for relatives.

Catholics further believe that Mary was "conceived immaculately" in the womb of her mother. The Immaculate Conception is not the same as the Virgin Birth, which refers to Christ's being conceived and born of Mary without human intercourse. The Immaculate Conception simply means that Mary was conceived in her mother's womb without original sin, or to state it positively, that from the first moment of existence, she was redeemed. Catholics believe finally that Mary's body was assumed into heaven by the power of God at the moment of her death. This is the doctrine of Assumption.

The scriptural source of Catholic beliefs concerning Mary is to be found at least implicitly in Luke 1–2. Official teaching places her in the first rank of redeemed Christians, not a "fourth person" of the Trinity, but a human being. Yet she was a human being loved by her son and raised to her dignity only because she was the perfect Christian, the one who best fulfilled Jesus' own idea of sanctity.

Pilgrimage in the World

The Catholic church encourages its members to enter into the life of the secular city and to exercise their rights of citizenship in their nation. It has lived with every kind of political situation from the time of the Roman Empire, through feudalism and monarchies, to the modern democratic form of government. As Vatican II reminded us, the church has the duty to build a better world based upon truth and justice. Since that council, a number of influential social teachings have promoted matters such as the dignity of every human being, the importance of human rights, and our solidarity with suffering people throughout the world. Christians on their pilgrimage toward the heavenly city should seek and savor the things that are above. At the same time, this only increases their obligation to work with all people in constructing a more human world.

For Discussion

□ Did you grow up with prejudice or misinformation about Catholic beliefs and practices? Talk about those.
□ The Roman Catholic Church is the "mother church" for most Western denominations. Do you see your own church as being more similar to the Catholics than different, or vice versa?
□ What are your own thoughts and beliefs regarding the authority of the pope, the status of Mary, and other points of difference? How important are those differences?

For Further Study

□ *Catholicism* by Richard McBrien (Minneapolis: Winston Press, 1990)
□ *Epiphany: A Theological Introduction to Catholicism* by Aidan Nichols (Collegeville, Minn.: The Liturgical Press, 1996)
□ Roman Catholic Web site: www.nccbuscc.org

Table of Comparison	*Roman Catholics*	*Lutherans*
Teachings	1. Believe in the triune God. 2. Believe in full divinity and full humanity of Christ. 3. Accept the Bible as the source of truth interpreted in the light of tradition. 4. Celebrate seven sacraments: Baptism, Confirmation, Penance, Eucharist, Marriage, Orders, and Anointing of Sick. 5. Believe in the real presence of Jesus in the consecrated bread and wine. The ultimate meaning of bread and wine are changed into the body and blood of Christ.	1. Same. 2. Same. 3. Accept the Bible as the source of truth expressed in creeds and confessions of tradition. 4. Celebrate two sacraments: Baptism and the Eucharist. 5. Believe in the real presence of Jesus in the Eucharist. Each communicant not only receives the bread and wine but also the body and blood of Christ.
Type of Worship	Mass celebrated in the language of the people. Two main sections: Word and sacrament. Order of Mass is the Western church pattern.	Liturgy is basically the same as Roman Catholic, but congregations have freedom to enrich the pattern.
Government	College of Bishops shares authority with the pope as head of College.	Interdependent congregational, regional, national, and global expressions of the church characterized by democratic decision making, strong ecumenical relationships, elected leadership, and an ordained ministry.
Characteristics	Priesthood restricted to males, who are forbidden to marry. Life and salvation includes the whole person—body and mind, believing and doing.	Men and women may become pastors (in most denominations); are allowed to marry. In practice, salvation tends to become more a matter of correct belief, less of doing.
Statistics*	Membership .... 61,207,914 Congregations .... 22,728 *U.S. statistics from *Yearbook of American and Canadian Churches 1998.*	

CHAPTER 29

The Salvation Army

The Salvation Army has, through the years of its existence, faced the changing and expanding problems in society while still keeping its evangelical intent in the forefront. Preserving its individuality in worship and methods, it has become increasingly involved in programs and services consistent with its purpose of ministering to the spiritual and physical needs of humanity.

The Salvation Army believes in the fellowship and unity of all believers, however, because of its particular organization, worship, and doctrine, the Army continues to hold to its identity as a church.

William and Catherine Booth believed that a hungry person must be fed before he or she will hunger for the Word of God.

Booth and "War"

The slums of London's East End moved William and Catherine Booth to dedicate their lives to the poverty-stricken and unchurched people of that area. Earlier, in 1861, as an ordained Methodist minister, William Booth had left the pulpit to become an evangelistic preacher. However, his confrontation with the slums in 1865 changed the course of his life.

The Booths initially intended to supplement the work of regular churches. All too often, however, converts were not accepted in these churches. The Booths soon found that rather than sending converts out of the area, they needed them to help handle the great crowds that attended their meetings. The work started under the name of the Christian Mission, but the name was changed in 1878 to The Salvation Army.

After the movement's name was changed, a new theme dominated the organization's work. A declaration of faith, called the "Articles of War," was developed. Booth was called a *General* and a quasi-military pattern of authority was formulated. Mission stations became corps, members became soldiers, evangelists became officers, and converts were called prisoners. Booth sought to develop an army of crusaders to save people in the "war" against evil.

Once committed to a "military" policy of expansion, Booth began to send officers and soldiers throughout the world. The Army quickly spread. Today, The Salvation Army works in 105 countries with about 25,000 officers who preach the gospel in some 160 languages at 15,670 evangelical centers. The Army also operates almost 9,000 social welfare institutions, hospitals, schools, and other centers.

Eleven Doctrines

The Salvation Army's constitution, originating in Christian Mission days, developed through a series of deed polls culminating in The Salvation Army Act 1980. This document gives The Salvation Army the legal status and power it needs to continue its work for the honor and glory of God. Included in the Act are the 11 cardinal doctrines of The Salvation Army, including the Army's affirmation of the Bible as the only rule of Christian faith and practice (God as Creator and Father of all). Other affirmations include: the doctrine of the Trinity; Christ's humanity and divinity; sin as the great destroyer of a person's soul and society; salvation as God's answer to the sins of humankind; hope available through Christ; the maturing experience of a life consecrated for the holy purposes of God's kingdom; and an eternal destiny of victory over sin and death. The Methodist beliefs of the founder are reflected in the group, including an emphasis on complete sanctification or holiness.

Although the Army functions both as a church and a social agency, its primary purpose is the salvation of humankind "by the power of the Holy Spirit combined with the influence of human ingenuity and love."

The Booths believed that the sacraments are not essential to the salvation of the soul; therefore the Army does not observe them. This feature of the Army significantly distinguishes this group from most of the other communities of belief within Christendom. Despite the Methodist heritage of the Army, the sacramental part of that tradition was lost.

Basic Training

Converts who want to become soldiers (members) of The Salvation Army must sign the "Articles of War." These articles are the conditions of membership. Enrollment as a member of the Army then occurs in a public ceremony. Volunteer service for Army work is expected of the new soldiers.

The function of The Salvation Army officers is similar to that of ministers in other denominations. These officers are ordained and commissioned for full-time service.

Vast Social Work

A significant program of social welfare is carried on by The Salvation Army and financed through the voluntary offerings of its members and contributions from the general public. The Booths' belief that a hungry person must be fed before he or she will hunger for the Word of God undergirds the practice of the Army even today. The importance of the social welfare program to the soldiers of the Army is clearly stated in the following excerpt from The Salvation Army Mission Statement.

> The Salvation Army, an international movement, is an evangelical part of the universal Christian church. Its message is based on the Bible. Its ministry is motivated by the love of God. Its mission is to preach the gospel of Jesus Christ and to meet human needs in His name without discrimination.

For Discussion

□ How do you react to The Salvation Army's quasi-military style?
□ The Salvation Army is best known for its social work. How important do you think such activity is for church bodies?
□ How do you react to the Army's nonuse of baptism and communion?

For Further Study

□ *Marching to Glory* by Edward H. McKinley (Grand Rapids: Eerdmans, 1995)
□ The Salvation Army Web site: www.salvationarmy.org

Table of Comparison	*Salvation Army*	*Lutherans*
Teachings	1. Accept the Bible as the Word of God. 2. Teach justification by faith. 3. Believe in the full divinity and humanity of Christ. 4. Do not observe sacraments.	1. Accept the Bible as the written witness to God's revelation of saving through Jesus Christ. 2. Teach justification by grace through faith. 3. Same. 4. Celebrate two sacraments as means of God's grace: Baptism and Holy Communion.
Type of Worship	Nonliturgical with much freedom for member participation. Simple, direct appeal to personal decision.	Liturgical, following classical form of Western church. Member participation in dialogue between pastor and people in worship.
Government	Quasi-military, authoritarian in structure but democratic in principle.	Interdependent congregational, regional, national, and global expressions of the church characterized by democratic decision making, strong ecumenical relationships, elected leadership, and an ordained ministry.
Characteristics	Major emphasis on evangelism, service, and Christian living; cautious about membership in other religious groups without doctrinal agreement; clergy permitted to marry if both parties are officers.	Emphasis on doctrine with Christian life to proceed from faith; increasing cooperation with other Christian groups; clergy permitted to marry without rules and regulations.
Statistics*	Membership .... 453,150 Congregations .... 1,264 *U. S. statistics from *Yearbook of American and Canadian Churches 1998*.	

CHAPTER 30

Seventh-day Adventist Church

Tithing, giving one-tenth of a person's income, in an important characteristic of the Seventh-day Adventist Church.

Adventists see in the events of the modern world continual reminders of Christ's challenge to discern "the signs of the times" (Matthew 16:2-3; see 2 Timothy 3:1-5). Expanded technology, burgeoning population, and social upheavals all contribute to this awareness for the Adventist.

Seventh-day Adventists believe that all sincere Christians constitute the invisible church, but they also believe that the Seventh-day Adventist Church has been given a special message to proclaim to the world in this generation. This special message is the everlasting Gospel of Jesus Christ and the announcement of Christ's return. The message calls for immediate preparation for what is believed to be Christ's imminent, personal, visible return to earth in glory and power to establish Christ's universal and eternal reign.

This church is a conservative Christian body, extending throughout the world. It considers itself evangelical in doctrine and professes no creed except the Bible.

Ill-fated Dating

Seventh-day Adventists doctrinally are heirs of the eighteenth and nineteenth century widespread interest in the second advent of Christ. Followers of evangelist William Miller expected Christ's return between March 21, 1843, and March 21, 1844. When the ill-fated dating proved incorrect, a later date was set, but again the day of the Lord failed to materialize as expected.

A series of conferences under the leadership of James and Ellen White and Joseph Bates led to the fusion of isolated groups of Sabbath-keeping Adventists in New York and New England. Between 1848 and 1850, most differences were resolved and the main outline of teachings and beliefs was formulated.

During the 1850s the elaboration of teachings and doctrines was developed. Most of this occurred in periodical articles and pamphlets on various Bible subjects, often written in response to the claims of their opponents. At the general meeting in 1860 at Battle Creek, Michigan, the denominational name of

Seventh-day Adventists was adopted. (The first part of the name reflects the belief that Christians are still bound to keep the seventh day of the week as the Sabbath; the second part refers to the *advent,* or coming, of Christ.) Then in 1863, a General Conference convened and framed the church constitution.

Unique Doctrines

The assumptions of the Adventists depend heavily upon the apocalyptic books of Daniel and Revelation. Some distinctive doctrines include: a two-phase ministry of Jesus Christ as humanity's High Priest in the heavenly sanctuary, an "investigative judgment" in the heavenly sanctuary prior to the second advent, esteem for the witness of Ellen G. White as a special messenger, and the messages of the three angels in Revelation 14.

In addition to these distinctive features of Seventh-day Adventist theology, Seventh-day Adventists are in basic agreement with all conservative evangelical Christians concerning a wide range of doctrinal beliefs.

Commandments as Response

Seventh-day Adventists believe that the Holy Scriptures of the Old and New Testaments were given by God's inspiration and contain a revelation of God's will to humanity. They believe the Bible's teaching about the Trinity, and they believe that the universe and the world were created and are sustained by God through Christ. The origin of the world was through the special creative acts of God in six days and not through a long evolutionary process. Because of sin humanity lost its original state of perfection, but by faith in Jesus Christ human beings may be saved—renewed and restored by the transforming power of the Holy Spirit to enjoy eternal life—all through the grace of God.

The church beliefs are in harmony with historic Christianity as expressed in the Apostles' Creed, but the church does not hold to any creed. Before candidates are received into church membership, however, they affirm a series of beliefs and practices of Seventh-day Adventists.

Baptism by immersion, Holy Communion and foot washing, tithing (a tithe is one-tenth of a person's income), and nonliturgical services are characteristic. Members tend to take religion personally and seriously in regard to time, possessions, and health. They eat and dress simply and avoid that which science has shown is harmful to mental and physical health, such as tobacco, alcoholic beverages, drugs, certain meats, and excesses of any kind.

They believe that salvation is a gift through faith in the righteousness of Christ. They keep the Ten Commandments in response to the love of Christ and his sacrifice on the cross.

State and God

Church members are increasingly active and involved in community health, welfare, and disaster programs.

Believing that people have a twofold duty to God and state, the Seventh-day Adventist Church affirms that God has delegated to civil government authority and jurisdiction in temporal, earthly matters; however, only God has authority and jurisdiction over a person's conscience. In the best interests of both church and state, it is believed civil government must observe strict neutrality in religious matters, neither promoting religion nor restricting individuals or the church in the legitimate exercise of their rights for religious freedom.

For Discussion

□ This denomination arose out of a belief that Christ would return very soon. How do you respond to people who hold such beliefs?
□ Though many Christians enjoy Saturday worship, how would you answer the claim that because of the Sabbath commandment that is the day on which all Christians *should* worship?

For Further Study

□ *The Seventh-day Adventists: A History* by Anne Devereaux Jordan (New York: Hippocrene Books, 1988)
□ Seventh-day Adventist Web site: www.adventist.org

Table of Comparison	*Adventists*	*Lutherans*
Teachings	1. Accept the Bible as the Word of God and believe in continuing spirit of prophecy.	1. Accept the Bible as the written witness to God's revelation of saving action through Jesus Christ. All subsequent revelation must be interpreted in light of God's central revelation in Jesus Christ.
	2. Accept the Trinity and the atonement of Christ.	2. Same.
	3. Practice Baptism, Holy Communion, and foot washing.	3. Celebrate sacraments of Baptism and Holy Communion.
	4. Regard observance of Seventh-day Sabbath as binding for all time.	4. Seventh-day Sabbath binding only for Old Testament times; Christ's resurrection celebrated each Sunday.
	5. Consider tithing and dietary rules binding on Christians.	5. Stress the freedom of the Christian under the gospel.
Type of Worship	Nonliturgical.	Liturgical.
Government	Local churches have considerable power, but a type of representative government is used for business of church.	Interdependent congregational, regional, national, and global expressions of the church characterized by democratic decision making, strong ecumenical relationships, elected leadership, and an ordained ministry.
Characteristics	Emphasize Christian education for all ages and healthful living through medical institutions and a variety of community-oriented health education programs.	Strong commitment to Christian education. Have program of missionary work also, but proportionately less active.
Statistics*	Membership . . . . 809,159 Congregations . . . . 4,363 *U.S. statistics from *Yearbook of American and Canadian Churches 1998.*	

CHAPTER 31

Unitarian Universalist

The lighting of a candle placed in a silver chalice is a central act of the worship service in many Unitarian Universalist congregations.

The history of Unitarian Universalism is a history of a religious people challenging the authority of the church, its creeds, and traditions. While these sources of authority were being challenged, the individual's ability to understand what is interpreted as the word of God, truth, right, and good was affirmed. Reason was also defended as the basic criterion for judging religious truth and understanding scripture.

The movement called Unitarian Universalism began as a series of disconnected efforts to complete the Reformation. Two points of focus were the Trinity and the divinity of Christ. In 1531 Michael Servetus, a Spanish radical, challenged the traditional doctrine of the Trinity, arguing that there is no *distinction of beings* in God but only *manifold aspects of deity*. Francis David in Transylvania (present day Romania) declared in 1569 that "the equality of Christ with God is only of a kind which God gave Christ, God remaining in his divine sovereignty above everyone else." The "unity" of God is preserved, leading to the name *Unitarian*.

During this period in the history of Christianity, differing points of view were not readily accepted in either the Roman Catholic or Protestant churches. An individual challenging the accepted view of the Church risked being labeled a heretic and exiled from particular areas. The church and the state were not separate, so decisions made by the church officials could affect the political rights of a citizen. A very important and radical step toward religious freedom was taken when Francis David convinced King Sigismund of Transylvania to enact the first edict of religious tolerance in 1568. Michael Servetus did not have this freedom and was burned at the stake for his beliefs in Geneva, Switzerland. He is considered the first Unitarian martyr.

Reason and Belief

Unitarianism later emerged in England again using reason in religious belief. Human reason was employed in the interpretation of Scripture, the purification of Christian doctrine, and the defense of religious liberty. John Locke, Isaac Newton, and Joseph Priestley (the leading spokesperson for Unitarianism as well as a noted scientist) were influential spokespersons for "the reasonableness of Christianity."

American Unitarianism, while influenced by European ideas, arose in New England as an indigenous movement of freedom of conscience and congregational independence. These Unitarians rejected doctrines such as predestination, total depravity, the Trinity, and eternal torment, while affirming a belief in the moral capacity of humans, the unity of God, the importance of reason, democracy in religion, and universal salvation. Its adherents opposed slavery as an insult not only to humans but to the God in whose image they were created. Ralph Waldo Emerson, the famous American literary figure, began his career as a Unitarian minister applying his ideas of transcendentalism to religion. His ideas were very influential in Unitarianism as he stressed the addition of intuition to human reason as a way of discovering religious truth.

Universalist Roots

Universalism developed in eighteenth century England. The conviction, rooted in 1 Corinthians 15:22 and other scripture texts, that God elects *all* humans to salvation was held in various forms by Origen of Alexandria, Gregory of Nyssa, and other church fathers. Universal salvation, abbreviated as Universalism, argued against the Calvinist belief that some are predestined to heaven and others are predestined to hell. John Murray is often credited with bringing Universalism from England to America at the end of the eighteenth century, although groups with universalist beliefs were present in America prior to his arrival. Universalism attracted thousands of converts on the American frontier during the nineteenth century.

The Unitarian and Universalist beliefs in a benevolent God and universal salvation gave them a common belief during the nineteenth century. In the twentieth century these two separate denominations worked toward a merger for several decades. This finally took place in 1961, resulting in the Unitarian Universalist Association.

Contemporary Attitudes and Practices

In accordance with the principle of individual freedom of belief, Unitarian Universalists hold widely varying convictions concerning themselves, their church, and the world. Within the circle, one can find Unitarian Universalist Christians, Buddhists, and pagans (embracing earth-centered spirituality), among others. Some of the most characteristic beliefs are summarized here.

Most Unitarian Universalists affirm God to be the evolutionary process by means of which the universe and humans came into being and tend toward perfection. For some, God is a reality to whom prayer is directed. For others, the word *God* is an abstract symbol for the unity of existence.

Unitarian Universalists regard Jesus as a human being. Some hold Jesus to be one figure in the line of world prophets extending from Moses and Buddha to Gandhi and Martin Luther King Jr. Christian-oriented Unitarian Universalists, a minority within the denomination, regard Jesus as the Christ who came to bring a new era to the world, an era whose vehicle is the church and whose consummation is reconciling love.

The church, for Unitarian Universalists, is an association of persons who choose to unite for worship, personal growth, and social outreach. Being congregational in organization, each local group has full authority to determine its teachings and call a minister.

Unitarian Universalist worship expresses the particular faith of each local congregation and its minister. There is no prayerbook, no liturgical year, no mandatory sacrament. The sermon occupies a large place in worship. Unitarian Universalists are flexible in their attitudes toward worship. Some pray to God, others ponder the events of the day, others unite in what one minister calls the *sacrament of silence*. Many congregations and ministers enjoy dialogue or discussion sermons, and the use of sacred dance, jazz music, and the graphic arts.

Active in Society

Unitarian Universalists have always been in the forefront of humanitarian initiative—historically in the abolition of slavery, the establishment of universal education, voting rights for all adults, and in efforts to improve the condition of the poor, the blind, and the mentally ill; today in the cause of peace, human rights, the right to choose abortion, separation of church and state, and gay rights. Unitarian Universalists ordain gay, lesbian, bisexual, and transgender ministers, and its General Assembly in 1996 passed a resolution supporting same-sex marriage.

Support of women's rights has long been a hallmark of the denomination. In fact, the Universalists were the first denomination to ordain a woman (Olympia Brown in 1863). The number of female ministers in the combined denomination dramatically increased in the late twentieth century, reaching 50 percent in 1999. This reflects a consistent denominational attitude toward the important role of women in religion.

Although excluded on doctrinal grounds from most councils of churches, Unitarian Universalists maintain active and cordial relationships with other denominations. The National Council of Churches is represented by official observers at the annual General Assemblies of the Unitarian Universalists Association. Ministers are active in interfaith activities at many levels of church life including ecumenical worship, study groups, and efforts for peace and social justice.

For Discussion

□ What would you consider to be the opposite of the Unitarian Universalist reliance on reason to determine belief?
□ How would you answer the Universalist claim that God saves all people?
□ In what ways do you think your denomination should follow the example of Unitarian Universalism? It what ways do you think it should not?

For Further Study

□ *A Chosen Faith* by John A. Buehrens and F. Forrester Church (Boston: Beacon Press, 1998)
□ *Pocket Guide to Unitarian Universalism* edited by William F. Schulz (Boston: Skinner House Books, 1993)
□ *Channing, Emerson, Parker: Three Prophets of Religious Liberalism* edited with introduction by Conrad Wright (Boston: Skinner House Press, 1986)
□ Unitarian Universalists Web site: www.uua.org

Table of Comparison	*Unitarian Universalists*	*Lutherans*
Teachings	1. The Bible is a book written by humans that must be understood in its historical context. 2. Creeds are rejected as a violation of reason, conscience, and experience. 3. The unity of God is affirmed. 4. Jesus is viewed as a great teacher and example, not a person of the Trinity. 5. Salvation by character: "You will know them by their fruits" (Matthew 7:16).	1. The Bible is the written witness to God's revelation of saving action through Jesus Christ. 2. Creeds are accepted as summaries of Christian truth. 3. The unity of the triune God is confessed. 4. Jesus is confessed as both divine and human in nature, the second person of the Trinity, our Savior. 5. Salvation by grace through faith, a gift of God: "The one who is righteous will live by faith" (Romans 1:17b).
Type of Worship	Worship is more of a celebration of the present than a memorial to the past. Historical and experimental forms are intermixed.	Worship is a celebration of God's grace and a confession of faith. Liturgical forms used to glorify and thank God.
Government	Freedom of individual conscience is secured in the independence of local congregations. Continental body is a democratic association of local churches and fellowships.	Interdependent congregational, regional, national, and global expressions of the church characterized by democratic decision making, strong ecumenical relationships, elected leadership, and an ordained ministry.
Characteristics	Regarding human nature as basically good, Unitarian Universalism appeals to their humane and progressive impulses. Strong in urban and university centers. Experience is regarded as the final test of truth.	Regarding human beings as sinful and in need of salvation, the Lutheran church proclaims the gospel in Word and sacrament. Although appeal made to all, its membership is largely middle class. The revelation of God in Christ is the primary truth to be received in faith.
Statistics*	Membership . . . . 213,342 Congregations . . . . 1,036 *U. S. statistics from the Unitarian Universalist Association.	

CHAPTER 32

United Church of Christ

Sponsoring homes for children is one way the United Church of Christ works for justice and love in society.

Formed in 1957, the United Church of Christ blends four distinct heritages within the Christian tradition "in order to express more fully the oneness in Christ of the churches composing it, to make more effective their common witness in Him, and to serve His kingdom in the world..." (Constitution of the United Church of Christ, 1960).

As a united and uniting church, it takes seriously the prayer of Jesus Christ "that they may all be one." It affirms God's intention to reconcile the whole world to God, and sees church unity as contributing to this larger purpose. This search for greater unity has led to the declaration of full communion with the Christian Church (Disciples of Christ), including the reconciliation of ministries, and to adopting the Formula of Agreement with other Reformed denominations and the Evangelical Lutheran Church in America. It further recognizes that the primary force for change in the world and in the church is the activity of God, however dimly perceived, as God continually creates, judges, and redeems the world in order to fulfill God's purposes. Thus, it dares to search for and respond to signs of God's activity for justice and reconciliation in secular events as well as in the movements toward unity within the life of the church.

As it focuses on God's work in our time, the United Church recognizes the importance of remembering how God has worked in the past, and how the church has attempted to be faithful through the centuries. It affirms the continuation of its own various traditions, as well as its solidarity with all Christians from the earliest times. At the same time it recognizes the need for continual adaptation of lifestyle and reformulation of doctrine in the church if it is to remain faithful to the good news of God in Christ. Thus it attempts to take its heritage seriously, not to preserve the past, but to discern the shape of hope for the future in order to live more faithfully in the present.

Four Streams of History

Two of the four major streams composing the United Church of Christ trace their distinctive roots back to Reformation times in Europe. A third stream originated in England during the early seventeenth century, while the fourth stream is of purely American origin, dating from about the beginning of the nineteenth century.

The first of the two European streams was that of the Reformed churches in Switzerland, in Germany, in France (the Huguenots), and in Hungary. Members from the German-speaking Reformed churches arrived in America in the early 1700s to form the German Reformed Church, later called the Reformed Church in the United States. These were followed during the next 200 years by immigrants from the other countries. One of the priceless heritages brought by these reformed people was the *Heidelberg Catechism,* written by Olevianus and Ursinus under the inspiration of Lutheran reformer Philip Melanchthon.

The second continental stream originated as a result of the Prussian Union of 1817 between the Lutheran and Reformed churches. During the 1830s and beyond, many members of these Evangelical churches, as they were called, emigrated to the United States to form the Evangelical Synod of North America. One of their earliest acts after organizing in the 1840s was the preparation of the *Evangelical Catechism,* a synthesis of the *Heidelberg Catechism* and Luther's Small Catechism.

While the roots of the Reformed and Evangelical heritage go back to Reformation times on the continent, the earliest forebears of the United Church to settle in this country were refugees and colonists from England. This third stream came from two chief groups: the Independents (later called the Pilgrims), who founded Plymouth Plantation in 1620; and the Puritans, who formed the Massachusetts Bay Colony in 1630. Growing out of the fusion of these two groups were the Congregational churches.

A fourth stream of influence in the United church developed during the late 1700s and early 1800s. Three different groups of churches emerged as a result of splits from the Methodists in North Carolina, the Presbyterians in Kentucky, and the Baptists in New England. Each of these groups was seeking to be faithful to what they held to be the essentials of New Testament Christianity. Within 20 years these three groups had entered into fellowship with each other, calling themselves the Christian Churches. Committed to unity in Christ, they affirmed the Bible as the sole source of tradition, dispensed with formal organizational structures, rejected doctrinal formulations including that of the Trinity, and sought to live out in their lives the teachings of Jesus, guided by his divine Spirit. Believer's baptism was accepted by them as normative (required) for entrance into the church, though persons baptized in infancy were not excluded from the fellowship.

Process of Union

For many years these four streams flourished separately on the American scene, with occasional contacts. Not until the 1930s, however, did these streams begin to flow together. In 1931 the Congregational churches and the Christian Churches joined together in a fellowship known as the Congregational-Christian Churches. Shortly thereafter, in 1934, the Evangelical Synod of North America and the Reformed Church in the United States united to form the Evangelical and Reformed Church.

Early in the 1940s informal conversations between the two newly formed denominations were held concerning the possibility of eventual union. Despite major differences, these two groups were very similar in their fundamental perceptions of what Christian faith and life was all about. Basic factors were a common recognition of the *sovereignty of God* over the church and over human traditions, and an *emphasis on human freedom*. Additionally, both groups were themselves the product of unions and had experience with the process's strengths and weaknesses.

Theological Stance

With such a diverse background, it should be evident that there is no one "theology" of the United Church of Christ; however, it does have a distinctive theological stance. It recognizes that theological formulations and systems are human attempts to state the significance of the gospel in terms that point beyond themselves to the working of God in history. It also recognizes that the theology one *lives* is more fundamental than the theology one *says*.

In a broad sense, one can describe the United Church of Christ as trinitarian in character. The great majority of its members would affirm the sovereign love of God, the lordship of Christ, and the working of the Holy Spirit as descriptive statements of one and the same God, though the meaning and importance of each of these statements would vary greatly from person to person.

Human beings are created in God's image, to live in fellowship with God and each other, and to exercise stewardship over the rest of creation. Human sinfulness arises from lack of trust in God, which separates people from God and from their neighbor. This separation is overcome only through God's initiative toward humanity, shown in Jesus Christ.

Humankind's proper response to God involves one's whole life. It is not merely agreeing with doctrine, nor is it a passive acceptance of God's grace; rather, it is a passionate involvement for the sake of justice and love among all people. Human beings do not earn their salvation by this involvement; this work is a liturgy of praise and thanksgiving for God's love.

The Church: Company of Committed

The church is seen not so much as a company of the "saved" but as a company of the committed; a pilgrim people who live by faith, free people who are servants of God in the service of humanity. The primary function of the church and of its members is, therefore, to serve humankind. As it does this, it witnesses to the redeeming love of God who is the source of all meaning and power.

As a community of faith, the church draws together in remembrance and hope to celebrate through its worship what God has done, is doing, and promises to do; to confess its lack of faith and its inadequate response to God's love; to ask for continued guidance, healing, and inspiration; and to offer again and again its resources for God's service in the service of humankind. Within the community its members share their varied experiences, nurturing one another in Christian faith and life, and organizing for common action in the world.

A Church within the Body

Within the general framework of such doctrine, the United Church gives concrete, institutional expression to the church in various ways. Organizationally, it recognizes itself as a distinct fellowship—a church—within the body of Christ. In this sense it is more than just a collection of local churches. It has its own integrity, symbolized by a constitution describing the free and voluntary relationships among the various groupings.

Normally membership requirements consist of Baptism—either infant or adult—and a public *ceremony of intention* to participate in the life of the church. Other requirements for membership vary from congregation to congregation.

There are four structural expressions of the church: *the local church,* which is understood to be the primary form of the church; regional groups of congregations called *associations,* which are responsible for the standing of ministers and churches; *conferences,* which are statewide or larger groupings of local churches and associations responsible for the wider mission of the church; and the *General Synod* and its related national instrumentalities, which oversee global and national mission. Each of these settings of the church is autonomous in the matters for which it is responsible, but each lives in covenant relationship with all the other expressions of the church, through elected representation, flow of information and opinions, program activities, and financial support.

Each local church elects its own governing body, which may be called a church council, consistory, or board, depending on the historic tradition of the congregation. In many instances boards of deacons, trustees, or elders are responsible for the spiritual life and fiscal affairs of the congregation. Ministers or pastors are called by vote of the entire congregation on the recommendation of pastoral search committees, with the assistance of the association or conference minister.

Priority Issues of Need

Officially, the United Church of Christ is committed to a course of active involvement in the social, cultural, and political issues of our time. In practice, however, the forms and the depth of this commitment vary greatly among the congregations.

Special attention is being given by the United Church, along with other denominations, to the priority issues of racism, poverty, the environment, sexism, homosexuality, peace and justice, and becoming a multicultural and multiracial church. The General Synod has recommended that a homosexual orientation not disqualify a candidate for ordination. Many local churches have declared themselves "open and affirming" regarding homosexuality. A number of gay and lesbian ordained ministers now serve in the United Church. Attempts in areas such as these are made not only to stimulate individual church members to appropriate witness and action, but to act corporately to enhance justice in the various structures of society.

The forms of action range from establishing and supporting traditional social service agencies such as hospitals, group homes, care facilities for the aged, and other treatment centers to participating in movements for neighborhood renewal, political action on justice issues in every kind of governmental jurisdiction, and advocacy for the poor, the oppressed, and those victimized whether because of gender, race, sexual orientation, handicapping conditions, or other circumstances. National boards and agencies of the church disseminate studies and strategies concerning these issues to local congregations so they can become agents of social change in their own communities, as well as help shape regional and national policy. It must be acknowledged, however, that since each church is free to determine its own program and stance, not all UCC congregations agree with national church agencies on these matters, and may choose to ignore or act against counsel from the wider church.

All too often the church acts as a privileged social institution rather than as the body of Christ committed to witness to God's love and justice and to serve humankind. Only continuing repentance and the restoration of God's forgiving and gracious love can transform the church into an expression of God's purposes in the world.

For Discussion

□ How does the United Church's understanding of the importance of social ministry compare with that of your own denomination?
□ Do you think this denomination's history as a joining of mixed church bodies is a strength or a weakness? Why?
□ "The primary function of the church and of its members is, therefore, to serve humankind." From your own perspective, would you agree or disagree with that statement? Why?

For Further Study

□ *Theology and Identity: Traditions, Movements, and Polity in the United Church of Christ,* ed. Daniel L. Johnson and Charles Hambrick-Stowe (Pilgrim Press, 1990)
□ United Church of Christ Web site: www.ucc.org

Table of Comparison	*United Church*	*Lutherans*
Teachings	1. No prescribed creeds. Statement of faith adopted but not binding. Teaching may vary from one congregation to another.	1. Use creeds, Catechism, and confessions as summaries of Scripture's teachings. Congregations teach in accordance with Lutheran confessions.
	2. Most accept the Trinity, but interpretations vary.	2. Accept the doctrine of the Trinity.
	3. Most accept sacraments as signs of God's blessing.	3. Accept sacraments as channels of God's grace.
	4. Believe Christ's presence is celebrated in Communion.	4. Believe in the real presence of Christ in the celebration of Communion.
	5. Most rely on Christ's redemption for salvation.	5. Teach that people are saved by God's love as revealed in Christ.
Type of Worship	No set form of worship. Ranges from nonliturgical to liturgical.	Liturgical forms based on ecumenical patterns of the Western church.
Government	Four structures: congregations, associations, conferences, and General Synod. Each autonomous in own sphere, but in covenant relationship with other expressions.	Interdependent congregational, regional, national, and global expressions of the church characterized by democratic decision making, strong ecumenical relationships, elected leadership, and an ordained ministry.
Characteristics	Strong stress on Christian living; much doctrinal freedom. Emphasis on church unity and cooperative movements.	Strong emphasis on doctrine with Christian life expected to proceed from faith in Christ. Individual and whole church to make faith active in love. Increasingly active ecumenically.
Statistics*	Membership . . . . 1,452,565 Congregations . . . . 6,110 *U. S. statistics from *Yearbook of American and Canadian Churches, 1998.*	

A FAMILY TREE OF DENOMINATIONS

Find the denomination at the bottom of the page and follow the line up to see where it developed from and approximately when. Some relationships are generalized. Denominations not connected to others bear no strong relationships in their development.

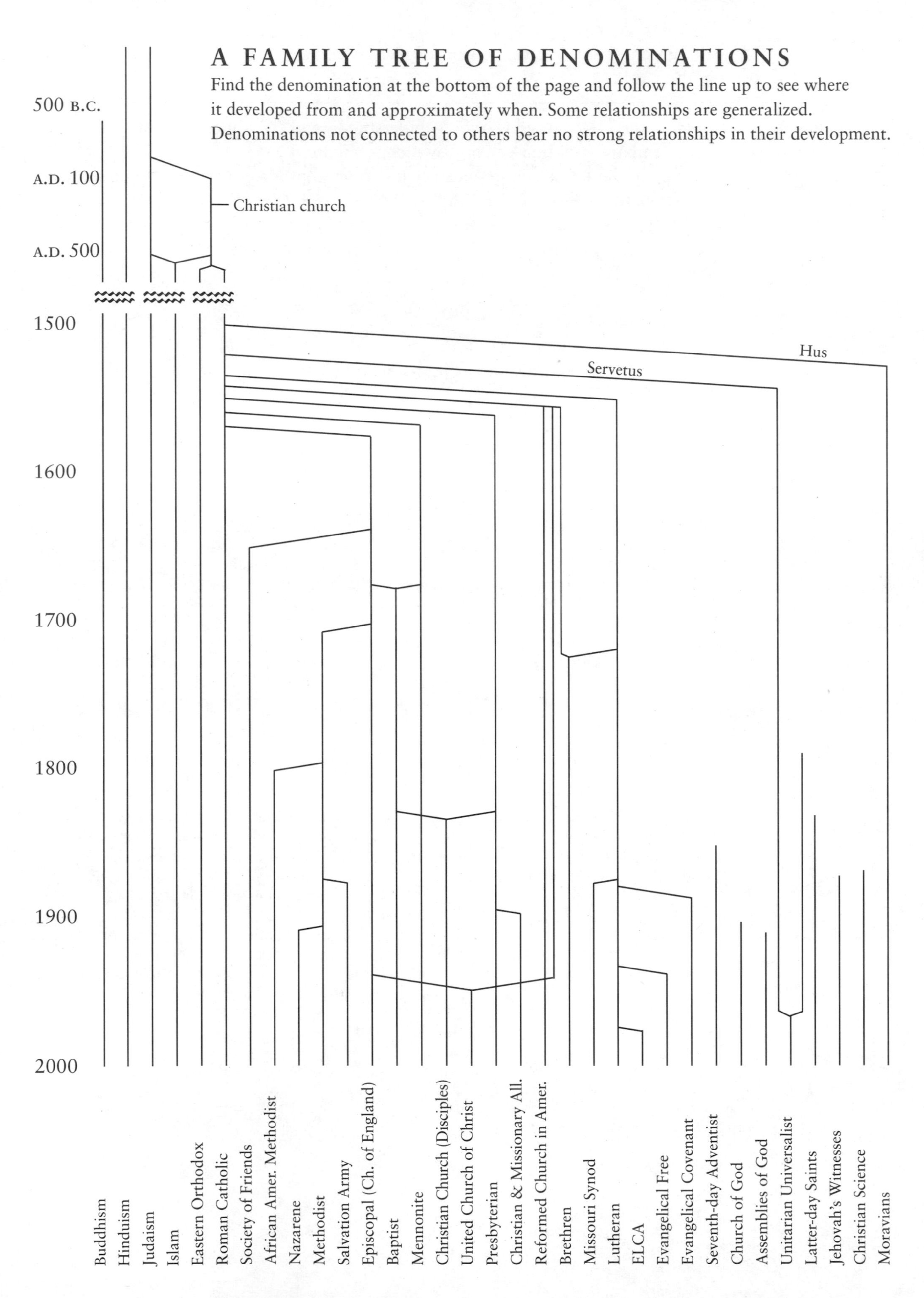